Estimating Economic Impacts of
Regulatory Changes to U.S. Port Operations

March 2007

Final Report

Produced for:
U.S. Coast Guard
Office of Standards Evaluation and Development
Standards Evaluation and Analysis Division
Washington, DC

Produced by:
U.S. Department of Transportation
Research and Innovative Technology Administration
Volpe National Transportation Systems Center
Cambridge, MA

DOCUMENT APPROVAL

Document Number of Final Version	Date of Document mm/dd/yyyy	Approver Initials	Date of Approval

DOCUMENT CHANGE HISTORY

Document Number	Version Number	Draft or final	Date of Document mm/dd/yyyy	Author's Initials	Author's Org	Description of Change

TABLE OF CONTENTS

TABLE OF TABLES

TABLE OF FIGURES

1. INTRODUCTION

This report describes a framework constructed to assist in understanding the long run impacts of regulations proposed by the US Coast Guard on domestic marine ports. The port impacts considered pertain to cost, time and reliability. These three factors have a direct bearing on demand for port services and should therefore be considered as part of an assessment of the consequences of proposed regulations. The role of ports in the global supply chain is significant and rapidly evolving. Actions taken through regulations that affect demand for port services have direct implications for international trade and, consequently, the nation's economic well-being.[1] These relationships are the subject of this report. As such, it forms part of an effort by the USCG Office of Standards Evaluation and Development to enhance the process of performing regulatory evaluations, as required by the White House Office of Management and Budget (OMB).[2]

This framework focuses on the container port sector of the overall port industry. This is done to make the analysis more manageable, but also in recognition of the fact that this sector has been the principal driver of the changes in ports and, as a result, supply chain management, over the last 20 years.

The last two decades have seen an unprecedented growth in the number and variety of goods traded internationally and arriving on U.S. shores. Spurred by the reduction of trade barriers, rapid economic development in Eastern Asia, and the growth of information technology, containerization has enabled the development of the tightly coupled system of goods movement that has become characterized as the global supply chain. These changes have put pressure on the nation's transportation and logistics systems, starting at the goods' place of entry, the port. U.S. ports today handle nearly 40 million TEUs[3] (twenty-foot container equivalent units) of container traffic each year.[4] This represents growth of 44 percent between 1999 and 2004.[5]

The increased use of containers has brought about new investment in port facilities, terminals, and technology. While these investments increase the ability of ports to compete with one another, there is reason to believe that this market is imperfect in an economic sense. The rise of China and Eastern Asia as trading partners has had effects on container traffic distribution, with port activity increasingly centered on the west coast

---

[1] The impact of regulations on port attributes, and hence port demand, are addressed here, along with the implications for trade. The analysis stops short of examining the implications on the economy as a whole. This is the subject of other ongoing research by the US Coast Guard.

[2] See http://www.whitehouse.gov/omb/circulars/a004/a-4 html for more on the regulatory analysis process as described in OMB's Circular A-4.

[3] American Association of Port Authorities, "North American Port Container Traffic – 2005," *AAPA Advisory,* May 8, 2006.

[4] This figure does not include "break-bulk," oil, gas, or RO/RO (automobile) imports, each significant sectors in their own right.

[5] U.S. Maritime Administration, *Containership Market Indicators,* Office of Statistical and Economic Analysis, U.S. Maritime Administration, available at: http://www.marad.dot.gov/marad statistics/ (Last Accessed: March 15, 2007), August 2005.

of the U.S. These shifts have put pressure on existing port operators, particularly in urban centers, and allowed new ports specializing in multimodal (ship-to-train) exchanges to enter the market. Shifting patterns of land use are also exerting pressure on ports. Existing ports are constrained in their expansion or other development by the market prices they face for the limited coastal land in urban areas (often competing with the "cappuccino crowd" for scarce waterfront locations). In addition, labor unions have incentives to slow the adoption of automation as a means of achieving the efficiencies that have become required to compete in the global market. Other constraints lead to externalities. The rapid increase in container traffic has brought with it congestion issues at and around the ports on all the modes that comprise the transportation network. This affects not only travel time, but creates environmental consequences, as well.

It is apparent from even this brief description of the modern port environment that anticipating the impacts of proposed government regulations, or the modification of existing ones, presents significant challenges. Safety and security continue to be priorities, and regulators continue to balance these concerns against the facilitation of the goods flowing through our ports, while ports operate in a highly competitive environment subject to complex constraints. The issues facing regulators are multiplied by the myriad agencies, Federal, state, and local, that have jurisdiction over port activities. Port operations fall under the purview of the U.S. Coast Guard, Customs and Border Patrol, other organizations within the Department of Homeland Security, the Environmental Protection Agency, state and local environmental agencies, and state and local transportation agencies.

Because of these issues, reform and refinement of port regulations must be an on-going process. While the port environment can be characterized as complex and dynamic, there is a set of three core attributes that are viewed from prospective users of port services: 1) the cost of moving a container through the port, 2) the time required to move a container through a port, and 3) the reliability of that movement, in terms of the ability to predict the schedule.

This report develops a systematic way to estimate the potential impact of a new regulation on these three core attributes. As the first step, ports can be described as a series of basic processes and characteristics. Port processes include, for example, lifting a container from a vessel, inspecting its contents, and stacking the container in the yard. Characteristics of the port include, for example, the length of the quay, the type and number of intermodal facilities, the size of the yard, and average calling vessel capacity, among others. These processes and characteristics will interact with each other in complex ways, depending upon local constraints.[6]

Next, potential regulations can be compared against the list of processes and characteristics to identify those processes that may be affected by the regulation. For instance, security changes reducing the number of dray truckers may reduce congestion at

---

[6] For instance, increasing yard size may decrease "digging" time as container stacks are shorter, but may increase movement time as yard trucks or straddle carriers have further to go. And such a trade-off between digging time and movement time is only possible where it is possible to increase yard size.

the gates but increase container dwell time and leave gantry crane operations completely unaffected. Effects are estimated for the three core port attributes (cost, time, and reliability) by the best means available. Port data are scarce and often proprietary. Estimating the impacts of a regulation on a port, and then inferring the response of the port, should use all the sources of information that are available.

The framework described thus permits a variety of techniques. The most rigorous techniques, from the standpoint of a regulatory analysis, involve using statistical and econometric methods. These methods require that sufficient data are available, but they are the most rigorous and thus adhere closely to OMB guidance. They have the added benefit that they capture the uncertainty of estimates as part of the analysis process.

When data are lacking, other methods must be employed. These are usually judgmental approaches, and include reasoning by analogy, "best-guess" estimates, or utilizing groups of experts. They are also capable of producing the required information. It may be more difficult to characterize and consistently track the uncertainty surrounding such methods, but it is possible.[7]

Approaches such as the Delphi method for extracting information from groups of experts, especially when paired with the Analytic Hierarchy Process (AHP),[8] have been employed in regulatory analyses and successfully conveyed the nature of regulatory impacts to decision makers and OMB. The methodology selection decision is best made on a case-by-case basis, given the constraints of time and budget, data available, expertise, previous changes in policy or practice, and the required degree of precision. This report will describe some of these methods as employed to illustrate the use of the regulatory impact framework.

For any specified situation, the changes in each of the three core attributes can be summed across processes and characteristics to find the overall effect that each proposed regulation would be expected to have on ports. Figure 1, on the next page, describes this process in graphical form.

The outline of the remainder of the report is as follows:

Section 2 provides a review of the literature relevant to port operation and efficiency (a detailed list of works reviewed and abstracts appears in Appendix A). This section highlights both the promising avenues of analysis that are currently being made in the literature, as well as some critical holes in current understanding. It then briefly describes the port industry; with a focus on geographic groupings that will be useful in determining what ports can be considered as peers for purposes of further analysis.

---

[7] The handling of uncertainty in the regulatory analysis as described in Circular A-4 is not as fully developed as that in Circular A-94, which provides guidance on Benefit-Cost Analysis. There has been continual movement in A-4 towards the practices described in A-94. The latter includes Monte Carlo analysis for treatment of uncertainty, a computationally intensive approach best left to data intensive cases where distributional assumptions can be tested.

[8] The Delphi method is described in Section 3.4.2 below and followed by a more general discussion in Appendix C. Analytic Hierarchy Processes are described in Appendix D.

Figure 1: The Port Attribute Assessment Process[9] [10]

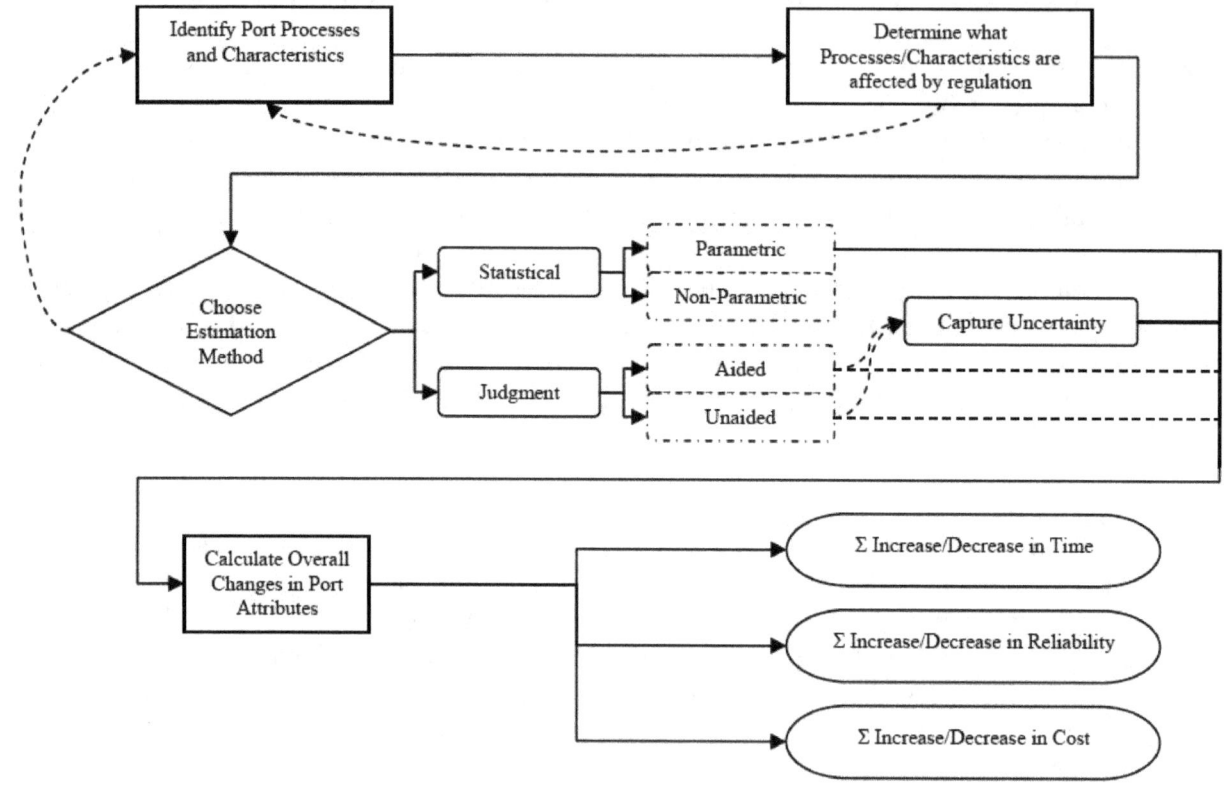

Section 3 then provides a detailed walkthrough of the analytical process shown in Figure 1, above. This section describes how to translate changes in regulation to changes in port attributes, and consequently, demand for port services. Section 3.4, on choosing estimation methods, includes discussion on surveying expert judgments and a statistical method to estimate changes in port characteristics, with a brief discussion on capturing uncertainty when using judgment techniques. A sample regulation relating to container stacking heights is included in the statistical section to illustrate the mechanics of the process.

Sections 3.5 and 3.6 continue the process of estimating overall changes in attributes and demand, maintaining the use of the statistical method outlined above and the example on container stacking heights.

Finally, Section 4 provides conclusions and recommendations on further research. It identifies places throughout the process where more complete and up-to-date information

---

[9] Dashed lines identify steps that are optional or conducted on an as-needed basis.
[10] Dashed boxes indicate that each box represents ends of a spectrum.

would allow for better estimates, more differentiated by port characteristics and geography.

Taken as a whole, this report identifies a process that can be used to estimate changes in port attributes and demand based on new regulations affecting port characteristics and processes. The general method can be adapted to suit the situation based on time, expertise, data, costs, and developments in the research. The latter, in particular, will help increase the usefulness of the analytic framework and support rigorous statistics-based estimates of regulatory impacts.

2. INDUSTRY AND ANALYTICAL BACKGROUND

Existing academic and professional research on port operations can be used to better understand the relationship between port characteristics and end-attributes. While evaluations of port efficiency are a popular sub-field of port research, the field has yet to come to overarching conclusions, or a standardized set of methodology.[11] There is, as yet, essentially no fully developed theory of the port. Econometric procedures are rarely applied to the study of ports, mainly, it appears, due to lack of sufficient data. Port simulations are more common. Simulations are driven by their assumptions, and tend to be looked upon with less favor in regulatory assessments than more statistically-based methods. Some researchers have attempted to use non-parametric methods, including data envelopment analysis (DEA), to calculate relative efficiencies among ports. Wang, Song, and Cullinane's (WSC) work in this area is perhaps the most complete.[12] They evaluate multiple DEA-based efficiency measures across 33 worldwide ports. Unfortunately, only three of the 33 ports studied by WSC are within the U.S.

The studies comprising the port literature remain far from comprehensive, and often are at odds with each other in terms of their results. Moreover, port level data for anything beyond basic information (throughput, number of cranes, land area), such as terminal fees, dwell times, and types/speeds of container handling vehicles are considered proprietary. Details on the sources and destinations of trade are spottily and reluctantly divulged, even to organizations such as the Institute of Shipping Economics and Logistics, which seeks the information for use in building its annual "Port Database" product.[13]

Citing work by WSC and others, the United States Maritime Administration (MARAD), concluded:

> …that it was unable to provide the requested comparison of the most congested ports in terms of operational efficiency due to a lack of consistent national port efficiency data. Given the diverse characteristics of U.S. ports, comparing port efficiency would require the creation of new methodologies and the collection of data that were not available for this report.[14]

To put this literature in context, a discussion of the port industry follows. Additionally, a brief review of the Coast Guard's regulatory authority as it relates to ports appears in Appendix B.

---

[11] For a listing of reviewed articles and their abstracts, see Appendix A.

[12] See, for example, Wang, Teng-Fei, Kevin Cullinane, and Dong-Wook Song, *Container Port Production and Economic Efficiency*, Palgrave MacMillan, Hampshire, United Kingdom, 2005. Also, Kevin Cullinane, *et al.*, "The Technical Efficiency of Container Ports: Comparing Data Envelopment Analysis and Stochastic Frontier Analysis," *Transportation Research Part A*, Vol. 40, 2006, p 354 – 374.

[13] Authors' correspondence with ISL Infoline database administrators.

[14] U.S. Maritime Administration, *Report to Congress on the Performance of Ports and the Intermodal System*, U.S. Maritime Administration, June 2005.

Competition among ports has increased to a point where there is quick response to changes in demand for their services.[15] The principal reason for this is the globalization of the container shipping market during the past twenty years, which has resulted in multiple choices for shippers, not just at ports specializing in trans-shipment, or serving as a "hub" for vessel routes, but also at ports designed to move goods into the hinterlands.[16]

Variability among port operations, and differences in how individual ports react to changes in the industry, resulting from endogenous trends or from regulation, stems from differences in port goals. The goals or objectives of a particular port in turn depend in part on the structure of port ownership. Ownership may be as a landlord, operator, or public/private venture. This gives rise to competing objectives, including maximization of profit, employment, throughput, or revenue. Achieving these goals requires ports to negotiate various prices with carriers. This has led analysts to observe:

> Pricing by ports and operators within ports is considered quite a complex and untransparant (sic) matter, and as such is sometimes perceived as archaic. This often results in debates about subsidies, captive markets, and ... questions concerning distortion of competition and/or abuse of monopolistic power.[17]

Ports now exist as part of a global supply chain, and although they are key nodes and obvious potential bottlenecks in the network, they are also likely to exert less pricing power than in the past. The efficiency of the global supply chain has transcended even geography. For example, due to the combination of West Coast port congestion and shifting relative costs, current global supply chain management practices are resulting in a reallocation of Asian container cargo from West Coast ports to the East Coast. As a result of this change, for instance, Savannah's container traffic has nearly tripled in the 10 years from 1993 through 2003.[18] Panama Canal container traffic increased 22% in fiscal year 2003, [19] and in 2004, the Port of Miami's most important trading partner was Hong Kong.[20]

Container ports come in various sizes, and it is often reported in the literature that there are scale economies in port operation. Thus, larger ports have a cost advantage over smaller ones. That does not mean that larger ports are necessarily more efficient, however. Throughput and technical efficiency (hereinafter referred to as efficiency), while related, are distinct concepts. Efficiency is the measure of the resources (i.e., port processes and characteristics) required to produce a given amount of output. Throughput is considered the output of a port for purposes of estimating cost and production

---

[15] See, among others, Malchow, Matthew B., and Kanafani, Adib, "A disaggregate analysis of port selection," Transportation Research Part E 40 (2004) pp., 317-337.

[16] See, for example, Song, *et al.*, "On cost-efficiency of the global container shipping network," *Maritime Policy Management*, January-March 2005, vol. 32, no. 1, pp. 15-30.

[17] From, Meersman, *et al.*, "Port Pricing: Considerations on Economic Principles and Marginal Costs," European Journal of Transportation and Infrastructure Research 3, no. 4 (2003), pp. 371-386.

[18] Long, Mindy, "Ship Lines Go East to Avoid California", *Transport Topics*, January 17, 2005, pp. 5, 22.

[19] Long, Mindy, "Ship Lines Go East to Avoid California", *Transport Topics*, January 17, 2005, pp. 5, 22.

[20] "East Side Story," *Inbound Logistics*, June 2005, pp. 34-40.

functions. Hence, a port is described as producing so many container movements per year, for example.

The top twenty U.S. ports in terms of their throughput (in TEUs) are shown in Figure 2, below. The top ports in shown in green. The next seven are indicated in blue, while the remaining ports are indicated in red.

The West Coast dominates container throughput, with Los Angeles and Long Beach together making up about 36% of the total U.S. throughput. The southeastern ports appear to be less space constrained, and therefore capable of greater potential growth, than the northeastern ports, which are usually quite urban (e.g., the ports of Boston, New York, and Philadelphia, among others, are located essentially in the middle of the city and are competing with other potential users for land and access). The Gulf ports tend to be oil ports, with container operations often secondary.

Figure 2: Ranking of Port Throughput in TEU (2005) [21] [22] [23]

---

[21] U.S. outline maps courtesy of www.theodora.com/maps, used with permission.

[22] Throughput from: American Association of Port Authorities, "North American Port Container Traffic – 2005," *AAPA Advisory*, May 8, 2006. San Francisco discontinued Container services as of 2005. Its 2004 numbers would have placed it number 20 on this list.

[23] For simplicity, 22 ports are considered in Figures and Tables in this report. They are the 21 ports evaluated in both the Turner *et al.* and the Blonigen and Wilson studies, plus Hampton Roads. These maps do not include Hampton Roads as the definition of the areas of the port varies from source to source (i.e. sometimes including all Virginia ports). In the throughput map, San Francisco is left off as it discontinued container operations in 2005, the most recent year of statistics. If San Francisco's 2004 volume was substituted into the map, it would have ranked 20th, just ahead of Galveston.

Figure 3 displays efficiency (as measured by Blonigen and Wilson),[24] and shows 21 ports,[25] the top seven of which are shown in green. The next seven are shown in blue, and the remaining seven are shown in red.

Comparing Figure 3 with Figure 2, Oakland, Los Angeles, and Long Beach are very efficient and have relatively high throughput. Seattle and Tacoma have relatively high throughput, but are nearly at the bottom with respect to efficiency. The newer southeastern ports (Miami, Charleston, Port Everglades, and Savannah) do not appear to be terribly efficient. One possible explanation for this is that the southeastern ports have recently expanded capacity in order to be well-positioned to handle higher throughput, but this has not yet resulted in significantly increased usage of the ports.

Figure 3: Port Efficiency Rankings (1991 - 2003)[26]

---

[24] Source: Blonigen, Bruce A. and Wesley W. Wilson, *Port Efficiency and Trade Flows*, Institute for Water Resources, U.S. Army Corps of Engineers, IWR Report 06-NETS-R-11, Arlington, Virginia, United States, November 2006.

[25] The port of San Francisco appears in Figure 3 but not Figure 2. Historically, it was very efficient, but in recent years the TEU of the port has dropped off to zero.

[26] Blonigen, Bruce A. and Wesley W. Wilson, *Port Efficiency and Trade Flows*, Institute for Water Resources, U.S. Army Corps of Engineers, IWR Report 06-NETS-R-11, Arlington, Virginia, United States, November 2006.

3. THE ASSESSMENT PROCESS

The process we describe here for assessing the potential effect of changes in the regulatory environment on the demand for containerized cargo shipping through U.S. ports consists of three steps. The first stage is to project the effect of proposed changes in the regulatory environment on physical characteristics of U.S. container ports and the terminals within them. These characteristics include their processes for handling containerized cargo, the volume and nature of containerized cargo itself, and the sizes and other features of container vessels they can accommodate.

The second stage is to estimate the effects of changes in these variables on ports' costs for processing containers through the various stages in moving from ship to land transport mode (or the reverse), the total time these processes require per container moved (or port dwell time), and the variance in container-processing times (a measure of ports' container-handling reliability). The final stage is to estimate the effect of changes in these three key attributes of ports' container-handling productivity on the demand for containerized freight shipments through ports.

Each stage in this process should focus specifically on the specific U.S. container ports likely to be affected by a proposed regulatory change, although many regulations adopted by the U.S. Coast Guard are likely to affect all U.S. ports nearly uniformly.

3.1. Overview of the Analytic Process

One useful way to envision the regulatory evaluation framework is as a series of matrices that transform a proposed regulation into changes in trade volumes and container flows through U.S. ports through a series of distinct steps. The elements of each matrix are parameters that describe the changes in a set of consequences or outputs that are expected to occur in response to an initial action or to the consequences of the previous step in the analysis. The values of these parameters can represent either absolute or proportional changes in a consequence that occur in response to an initial action or previous consequence.[27] As the following sections indicate, estimates of these parameter values can be obtained from a variety of sources, and the source likely to provide the most reliable estimates can differ at each stage in the process.

The first step is to develop a matrix of changes in the physical characteristics of U.S. container ports' inputs and production processes that are expected to result from a proposed regulation. This is inherently a process relying heavily on the expertise and judgment of analysts familiar with the regulatory environment, the physical configuration

---

[27] In the former case, these parameters technically represent derivatives of the consequence variables with respect to each of the action or input variables, while in the latter case they represent elasticities. An elasticity is defined as the percent or proportional change in a variable that occurs when another variable affecting it changes by a given proportion or percentage. Elasticities have the advantage that they can sometimes be assumed to be independent of the initial values of the action (or input) and consequence (or output) variables.

of container ports and the cargo-handling processes they employ, and the competitive pressures that affect the form and speed of ports' behavioral adaptations to new regulations.

In the second step, this matrix is multiplied by others that translate the changes in ports' input and process characteristics into resulting impacts on their container-processing efficiency, the continuity of container flows through their cargo-handling processes, and the productivity with which they employ labor, equipment, facilities, and physical space (both water and landside). Changes in some inputs or processes required by new regulations will affect only ports' container-handling efficiency, process variability, or productivity in input use, but other regulation-mandated changes in inputs or processes may affect all of these variables. The preferred sources for parameter values summarizing these relationships are statistical measurements of container port efficiency and its determinants, econometric analyses of characteristics affecting ports' factor productivity, and simulation studies examining variability in ports' container-handling processes.

The subsequent step is to employ an understanding of how efficiency, reliability, and productivity are measured to translate changes in these variables into the response of port demand attributes, including fees or tariffs, container processing or dwell times, and the variance of processing times. Because efficiency is commonly measured in equivalent containers of a standard size (TEU) handled per unit of time (hour, day, year, etc.), any reduction in ports' container-processing efficiency as measured by this metric is directly translated into an equivalent change in its reciprocal, processing time per container or dwell time.[28]

The effect of regulation-induced changes in uniformity of container processing times on the variability of dwell time also depends on the units in which both are measured. However, these measures are less standardized in research, so informed judgment will be required to translate changes in one into its probable consequences for the other. For example, if simulation studies show that changes in ports' operating procedures required by a proposed regulation would increase the variance of container flows per unit time, this should be reflected in a proportional increase in dwell time variance. In contrast, if simulation results are reported as the frequency with which specific dwell time thresholds will be exceeded, these need to be "mapped" into increases in the variance or some other suitable measure of dwell time reliability.

Changes in factor productivity resulting from ports' compliance with new regulations are related to changes in port costs, although this relationship is slightly more complex. Simultaneous reductions in the productivity of all production factors mean that current container throughput can be only be sustained by increasing a port's use of all production inputs, which increases processing costs in direct proportion. In contrast, when a regulation reduces the productivity with which ports can use any single input, the increase in processing costs depends on both the decline in productivity and the share of

---

[28] Thus the elasticity of dwell time with respect to efficiency is -1; that is, a one-percent decline in efficiency leads to a one percent increase in processing or dwell time.

ports' total processing costs accounted for by that input. In either case, competition among U.S. ports for container traffic flowing between most U.S. and world origin-destination pairs appears to be sufficiently robust that increases in ports' processing costs will be fully reflected in increased fees or tariffs levied for any specific activity or service (unloading, transfer, storage, etc.) where productivity has been reduced.

Finally, changes in fees, mean or expected processing time, and its variance can be translated into port-specific estimates of changes in containerized cargo shipping demand using demand elasticities for these attributes. Econometric estimates of these parameters reported in published research are probably the most reliable, but even these are subject to wide uncertainty. They will also differ greatly depending on whether they incorporate reallocation of cargo movements among individual U.S. container ports in response to a proposed regulation's differential impacts on specific ports, or simply represent the response of total U.S. containerized cargo trade to changes in average attribute values at all U.S. ports. Estimated elasticities of container shipping demand at individual ports are not widely available, but are likely to be many times larger than those for total containerized cargo trade.

The following sections explore each of these steps in more detail. They also illustrate the evaluation of a sample regulation using parameter estimates drawn from published studies of container port efficiency, port fees, and the response of containerized trade volume to port charges.

3.2. Identifying Critical Port Processes and Characteristics

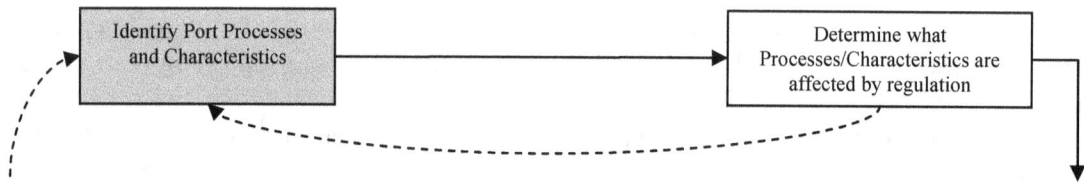

The process of identifying port processes and characteristics is fairly straightforward, and will only need to be done once if the list is sufficiently comprehensive. In a short turnaround situation, this step and the determination of the processes and characteristics that are affected by a regulation could be combined. However, in building a long-term, repeatable process, having thoroughly worked through this list can save time over the course of multiple regulatory assessments. A consolidated sample of such a list is shown in Table 1.

These tables can be generated for each U.S. port, and then sorted by a variety of port characteristics for different types of regulations. That is, a combined list could be made from the information on all publicly-owned ports, ports on the Gulf Coast, ports in urban centers, etc., or any combination thereof. In a time-constrained situation, one could begin at the aggregated level, if necessary.

Table 1: Port Processes and Characteristics

			Baseline	
			Time / Fee / Value	Reliability
Arrival				
	Ship Arrival			
		Number of Berths		
		Fees (per Vessel)		
		Fees (per Container)		
	Container Crane			
		Number/Reach of Cranes		
		Crane / Stevedoer / Wharfage Fees		
Stacking				
	Lift to Stack			
		Container Handling Vehicle		
		Handling and Other Fees		
	Storage			
		Stacking Space		
		Demurrage		
Inspection				
	Inspection			
		Open/Close Container		
		Facilitation Fee		
Departure				
	Truck			
	Truck Departure			
		Number of exit gates		
		Handling and Other Fees		
		Equipment Interchange Receipt		
	Train			
	Move to Railyard			
		Handling and Other Fees		
	Train Depart			
		Number of Class 1 Railroads		
		Equipment Interchange Receipt		
Throughput				
	TEU Unloaded per Vessel			
	Weight of Containers			
	Value of Goods			

3.3. Determine What Port Processes and Characteristics are Affected by a Regulation

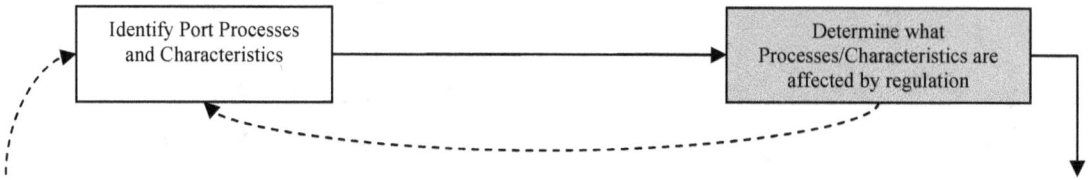

Any proposed regulation is likely to affect only certain port processes or characteristics. For example, a regulation that decreases the speed at which containers are inspected will affect stacking space, dwell time, and demurrage fees, but is unlikely to affect vessel queuing or unloading. Alternatively, if the inspection time becomes more variable, it may affect intermodal transfers to trains as well as train departures, since making up consists may take longer. Truck departures may be unaffected, as they are more resilient to any changes in container dwell times.

Identifying what is unaffected by a proposed rule can sometimes be just as valuable as knowing what will be. It will help identify (1) the relevant stakeholders, (2) those who have the most to gain or lose, and (3) the area experts that should be involved in the rest of the process. This activity may also identify processes or characteristics inadvertently overlooked in the previous step of the process (as recognized by the dotted line back to step one in the Figure).

In most cases, the majority of processes and characteristics will be unaffected by a proposed regulation and the list generated in Step 1 will become much smaller. For instance, as shown in Table 2, a sample regulation prohibiting stacks of containers only affects a small portion of characteristics and processes (the ones not affected have been shaded).

Table 2: Processes and Scenarios

			Baseline		Stacks	
			Time / Fee / Value	Reliability	Change in Time / Fee / Value	Change in Reliability
Arrival						
		Ship Arrival				
		Number of Berths				
		Fees (per Vessel)				
		Fees (per Container)				
		Container Crane				
		Number/Reach of Cranes				
		Crane/Stevedoer/Wharfage Fees				
Stacking						
		Lift to Stack				
		Container Handling Vehicle				
		Handling and Other Fees				
		Storage				
		Stacking Space				
		Demurrage				
Inspection						
		Inspection				
		Open/Close Container				
		Facilitation Fee				
Departure						
	Truck					
		Truck Departure				
		Number of Exit Gates				
		Handling and Other Fees				
		Equipment Interchange Receipt				
	Train					
		Move to Railyard				
		Handling and Other Fees				
		Train Depart				
		Number of Class 1 Railroads				
		Equipment Interchange Receipt				
Throughput						
		TEU Unloaded per Vessel				
		Weight of Containers				
		Value of Goods				

3.4. Choice of Estimation Method(s)

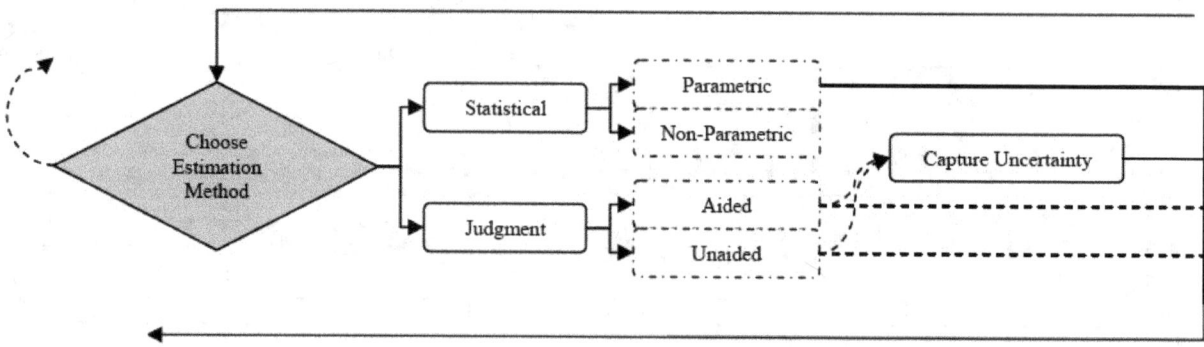

As noted earlier, the choice of estimation methods will depend on many considerations. These include time to perform, budget, the availability of experts or data, and the required degree of precision. In many situations, the statistical approach (parametric, non-parametric, or semi-parametric) will be the most desirable, as it can provide quantitative estimates of impacts and their associated degree of error. However, it also requires a large amount of data and agreed upon models of the processes under study. In cases where little data exist (e.g., in the case of a regulation with no precedent), the use of expert judgment can likely be more accurate than other methods. Such an approach can make use of aided approaches like the Delphi method for aggregating opinion and for consensus-building. Unaided approaches may also be used. In both cases, it is useful as part of the regulatory evaluation process to capture the underlying uncertainty associated with the data gathered. This can be done by representing estimates in a triangular distribution, which uses an upper and lower bound around the mid-point describing the most likely value.

Any other option that generates useful results should also be considered as the situation requires. One such method is simulation. While using a simulation can allow for many of the advantages of statistical methods, producing quantitative results along with measures of uncertainty, such an approach must also be employed with care. First, the results of simulations may be viewed with skepticism when the underlying calculations and assumptions are unclear. Additionally, in the case of ports, as described above, accurate simulations would require a degree of data accuracy and precision in assumptions that are not likely to be available with the current state of the literature.

3.4.1. Statistical Approach

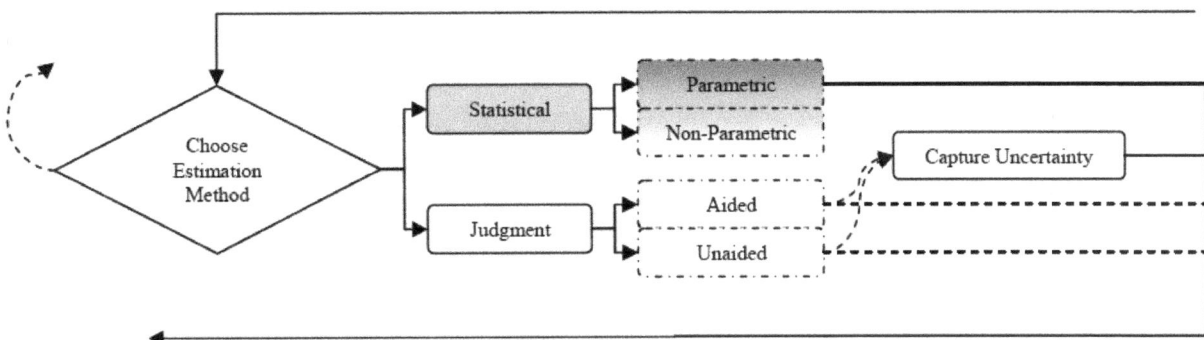

Statistical methods can be considered along a spectrum ranging from completely parametric to non-parametric. Most traditional econometric analysis is considered parametric, that is, data are employed with the assumption they fit known statistical distributions. In situations where full parameterization is possible, analysts can move along the spectrum to use other methods, including bootstrapping, Bayesian analysis, and Monte Carlo methods. Fully non-parametric approaches, like Data Envelopment Analysis (DEA), are also available. In the framework that follows, a combination of parametric and non-parametric methods is used.

Citing data difficulties outlined by MARAD (see above), Blonigen and Wilson[29] attempted to improve the assessment methodology. Their model, which is more detailed than many previous analyses, enables them to take into account the volume and types of cargo moving into a port. However, it still treats the characteristics and processes within the port as a "black box," and captures their combined effects in the form of a port-by-port adjustment factor. Furthermore, limitations on computational power and speed necessitated that their model be calibrated separately for each year in the sample, rather than using one combined model.

Turner, *et al.*, seek to better understand the factors affecting port efficiency by first developing a statistical measure of port efficiency.[30] Next, they use regression analysis in an attempt to isolate the contributions of individual port characteristics to differences in their measured efficiency.[31] Despite the inclusion of 13 port characteristics and

---

[29] Blonigen, Bruce A. and Wesley W. Wilson, *Port Efficiency and Trade Flows*, Institute for Water Resources, U.S. Army Corps of Engineers, IWR Report 06-NETS-R-11, Arlington, Virginia, United States, November 2006.

[30] Turner, Hugh, Robert Windle, and Martin Dresner, "North American Containerport Productivity: 1984 – 1997," *Transportation Research Part E*, Vol. 40, 2004, p. 339-356.

[31] The authors use data envelopment analysis (DEA) to develop their measure of port efficiency. DEA estimates the maximum container throughput that can theoretically be produced for each port's combination of land, capital, and labor inputs, and assesses each port's efficiency by comparing its actual output to the maximum attainable with its actual combination of inputs.

indicators to control for yearly shocks, they still find significant port-specific effects that cannot be accounted for by the included characteristics. Thus, while the particular black box in Turner, *et al.*, may be smaller than the one in Blonigen and Wilson, there are still a number of unexplained factors affecting port efficiency.

While there is little agreement on the method to be used to calculate overall efficiency, there is agreement that the physical characteristics of the port (number of berths, channel depth, number of cranes, etc.) and the makeup of cargo (number of containers, final destinations, etc.) are necessary ingredients in predicting efficiency. Using these common characteristics, published estimates of their effect on port productivity, and the judgment of experts, policymakers can begin to predict changes in attributes that are likely to result from new regulations. Moreover, the quantitative method outlined in this paper can be updated to reflect changes in estimates as the literature develops.

Tables 3 through 8 illustrate the regulatory assessment process, using statistical estimates of the relevant parameters drawn from the previously cited studies by Blonigen and Wilson and by Turner, *et al.* These parameters describe the relationships among (1) port characteristics and processes likely to be affected by the regulatory environment, (2) port operating efficiency or productivity, (3) port attributes such as container processing cost and dwell time, and finally (4) port demand and container throughput measures.

Table 3 identifies the characteristics of container cargo, ports and terminals, vessels, and container-handling processes that were found to affect port productivity in the analysis by Turner *et al.* Cargo characteristics include a port's total container throughput and average container volume processed per terminal, as well as the proportion of outbound containers arriving by feeder barge (rather than on land by truck or rail). Port characteristics include the fraction of port land area dedicated to container operations, percent of dock area with direct ship-to-rail connections, number of large railroads serving the port, where rail access offers adequate clearance for double-stacking of containers, and the maximum reach of container cranes.

Characteristics of vessels using each port include average container-carrying capacity, a measure of maximum vessel draft, and the fraction of containers carried on vessels with roll-o/roll-off capability. Port process characteristics are limited to the average number of days per year in which container operations are interrupted by work stoppages or other events.

Table 3: Elasticities of Port Productivity with Respect to Port Characteristics

Port Name	State	U.S. Region	Elasticity of Port Productivity with Respect to Characteristic:											
			Port Throughput (million TEU/yr.)	Avg. Terminal Throughput (million TEU/yr.)	Barge Feed (% of arrivals)	Container Operations (% of port area)	Direct Rail Access (% of dock)	Avg. Vessel Capacity (thousand TEU)	Maximum Vessel Draft (feet)	Roll-On / Roll-Off Operations (% of arrivals)	Double-Stack Clearance (yes/no)	Class I Railroad Service (number)	Mean Crane Reach (meters)	Processing Interruptions (Days/yr.)
Baltimore	MD	Northeast												
Boston	MA	Northeast												
Charleston	SC	Southeast												
Galveston	TX	Gulf												
Houston	TX	Gulf												
Hampton Roads	VA	Southeast												
Jacksonville	FL	Southeast												
Los Angeles	CA	West												
Long Beach	CA	West												
Miami	FL	Southeast												
New Orleans	LA	Gulf												
New York / New Jersey	NY, NJ	Northeast												
Oakland	CA	West												
Port Everglades	FL	Gulf												
Philadelphia	PA	Northeast												
Portland	OR	West												
Savannah	GA	Southeast												
Seattle	WA	West	0.134	0.259	0.013	0.000	-0.017	-0.233	-0.041	-0.024	-0.008	0.090	-1.439	0.001
San Francisco	CA	West												
Tacoma	WA	West												
Wilmington	DE	Northeast												
Wilmington	NC	Southeast												

Table 3 also reports sample elasticity estimates of container-processing efficiency with respect to each of these port, cargo, vessel, and process characteristics for the Port of Seattle. These are derived from the statistical model estimated by Turner *et al.*, together with data on these variables obtained from various government and industry publications.[32, 33]. As these sample values illustrate, port productivity is only modestly sensitive to changes in most of these characteristics; larger total container throughput volumes and throughput per terminal lead to increased productivity, as do a higher fraction of containers arriving by barge (rather than by truck or rail) and increased railroad service. The resulting higher productivity results in lower average costs for ports processing larger container volumes, relying heavily on barge transshipping, or with increased rail access.

Surprisingly, certain other port and vessel characteristics appear to reduce efficiency in container port operations, although some of these estimated effects are statistically unreliable. These characteristics include vessel size and maximum draft, fraction of roll-on and roll-off operations, clearance enabling double-stack operations, and longer crane reach. While some of these results cannot be ruled out on theoretical grounds – for example, extremely large vessels may prevent efficient utilization of ship berths or complicate container loading operations in ways that actually reduce productivity – others seem more difficult to explain. In practice, it will probably be desirable to utilize a combination of statistical estimation and other procedures, such as by replacing statistically estimated parameters that represent counter-intuitive effects with expert-based estimates of these effects.

Tables 4, 6, and 8 illustrate how the parameter estimates reported in Tables 3, 5, and 7 can be used to assess the impacts of a proposed regulatory change on port efficiency or productivity. In turn, the resulting changes in port productivity will affect port attributes (container-handling charges, container processing time, and processing time reliability), and through these attributes, demand for container shipping and container-port throughput. First, Table 4 gives estimates of the changes in physical characteristics of container cargo, ports and terminals, vessels, and container-handling processes resulting from a hypothetical regulation. The sample regulation would restrict container stacking heights in order to facilitate random container inspections, or to facilitate rapid physical isolation of containers with unidentified and possibly suspicious contents.

---

[32] Using elasticities to measure the sensitivity of changes in port productivity, port attributes, and container shipping demand to regulation-induced changes in port characteristics or processes expresses these results as proportions or percentages. (This is because elasticities measure the proportional or percentage change in variable that results from a given proportional or percentage change in a factor that influences it.) However, the analysis could also be conducted using measures of the *absolute* changes in productivity, port attributes, and shipping demand resulting from changes in port characteristics and processes in response to regulatory changes.

[33] The authors were unable to provide their original data to enable these calculations for all ports included in Table 3.

Table 4: Changes in Port Characteristics Resulting from Sample Regulatory Change

Port Name	State	U.S. Region	Percent Change in Port Characteristic:			
			Port Throughput	Avg. Terminal Throughput	Direct Rail Access	Processing Interruptions
			(million TEU/yr.)	(million TEU/yr.)	(% of dock)	(days/yr.)
Baltimore	MD	Northeast	-10%	-10%	-20%	5%
Boston	MA	Northeast	-10%	-10%	-20%	5%
Charleston	SC	Southeast	-10%	-10%	-20%	5%
Galveston	TX	Gulf	-10%	-10%	-20%	5%
Houston	TX	Gulf	-10%	-10%	-20%	5%
Hampton Roads	VA	Southeast	-10%	-10%	-20%	5%
Jacksonville	FL	Southeast	-10%	-10%	-20%	5%
Los Angeles	CA	West	-10%	-10%	-20%	5%
Long Beach	CA	West	-10%	-10%	-20%	5%
Miami	FL	Southeast	-10%	-10%	-20%	5%
New Orleans	LA	Gulf	-10%	-10%	-20%	5%
New York/New Jersey	NY,NJ	Northeast	-10%	-10%	-20%	5%
Oakland	CA	West	-10%	-10%	-20%	5%
Port Everglades	FL	Gulf	-10%	-10%	-20%	5%
Philadelphia	PA	Northeast	-10%	-10%	-20%	5%
Portland	OR	West	-10%	-10%	-20%	5%
Savannah	GA	Southeast	-10%	-10%	-20%	5%
Seattle	WA	West	-10%	-10%	-20%	5%
San Francisco	CA	West	-10%	-10%	-20%	5%
Tacoma	WA	West	-10%	-10%	-20%	5%
Wilmington	DE	Northeast	-10%	-10%	-20%	5%
Wilmington	NC	Southeast	-10%	-10%	-20%	5%

While the estimated magnitudes of the effects shown in Table 4 are only approximate, they indicate that such a regulation would be expected to reduce throughput at container terminals and thus for the port in total. By requiring more surface area for container storage, a limitation on stacking heights would also be expected to cause reallocation of some dock space from rail access to container storage. It might also slightly increase days lose due to container processing interruptions when inspections identify containers requiring isolation and further analysis. As Table 4 also shows, these regulatory impacts are hypothesized to be uniform (in percentage terms) across all ports in the sample, since any restriction on container stacking heights or procedures would presumably apply to all U.S. container ports.

The next section addresses alternative methods of estimating the effects of changes in port characteristics on port productivity or efficiency. Following section 3.4.3, the discussion of how statistical estimates of the relevant parameters can be used to estimate overall changes in port attributes and demand resumes.

3.4.2. Judgment Methods

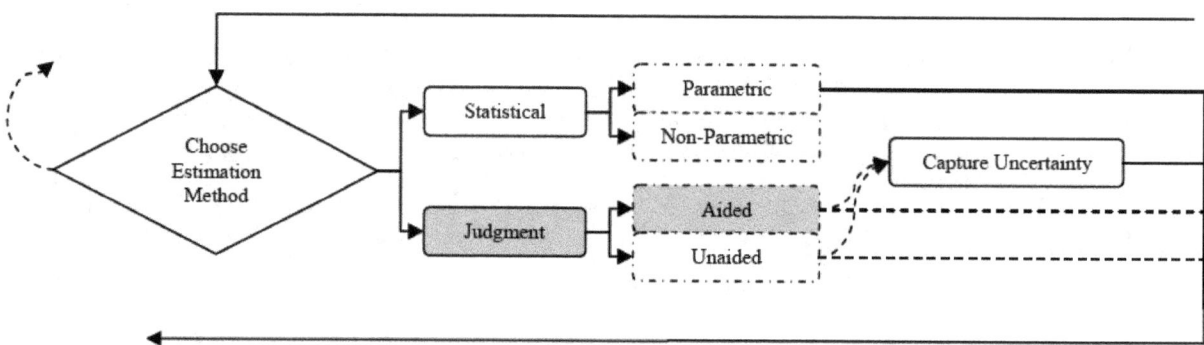

In cases where data do not exist or are otherwise unavailable, statistical methods of analysis may be difficult to apply. For example, this could be expected if a proposed regulation seeks to address a sufficiently rare event (e.g., finding a weapon of mass destruction within a port), to affect previously unregulated aspects of port activity, or to require processes and characteristics that are new to the port system. In these situations, the opinions of subject matter experts are likely to be more accurate than other methods, and reliable procedures for surveying experts and aggregating their judgments are required.[34]

Judgmental methods exist along a spectrum of aided to unaided approaches. One common aided approach is the Delphi Method. (For a discussion on the basics of the Delphi Method, see Appendix A.) This section continues with an example as to how the Delphi Method might be applied and is then followed with a discussion on how to capture some of the uncertainty around the estimates in a way that allows comparison with parametric statistical methods.

First, a group of decision makers is convened. The makeup of the group should encompass a broad range of backgrounds that include expertise on the port characteristics and processes, the proposed regulations, as well as relevant stakeholders.

The facilitator will present to the group the details of the regulation and an overview of the affected port(s), allowing anyone to ask questions. Once everyone has a sufficient grasp of the scenario, all group members will be asked to individually and anonymously rate expected impact on the characteristics or processes at question. Participants will be

---

[34] More on judgmental methods can be found at their professional organization, the Society for Judgment and Decision Making with a website at http://www.sjdm.org/ .

able to justify their choice in two or three sentences. In cases where participants have entered extreme values (two standard deviations away from the mean answer, for example), they will be strongly encouraged to justify their response.[35]

After all responses have been collected, the facilitator distributes a summary of the results. Depending on the group size, this may be a list of all responses, a frequency distribution of responses, or other descriptive statistics. The summary should also include the justifications for particular values, with particular importance on the reasons for answers far from the average. Participants will have the opportunity to read over the results and send back comments. These comments can be general or specific responses (positive or negative) to the justifications of others' answers. As all answers and comments are anonymous, comments need not be related to the participant's original answer. In fact, if a particular justification has swayed his or her opinion, a response noting why this is the case would be highly encouraged.

After sufficient time, the facilitator collects the responses and distributes them to the group, again anonymously. At this point, participants will have the opportunity to enter a new response for the affect of a regulation. For a second time, all participants are able to offer supporting comments, with special encouragement to do so for those with views outside the norm. The comments are distributed and the process repeats until a consensus is reached. Ideally, it should take two or three cycles for the consensus to emerge, though it is prudent to continue the process as long as opinions continue to shift from cycle to cycle. Unresolved significant differences of opinion among the experts may result in the need to develop a tie-breaking strategy, such as a vote.

The method just described can be partially automated, with software presenting each participant with a relevant dialog boxes. While all participants would still be able to enter justifications for their answers, the software could require justifications from those whose answers are significantly different from the average respondent (criteria could include two standard deviations or changes greater than 10% from the current situation, depending on the size of the group and the dispersion of responses). The combination and redistribution of the answers would be faster when done by computer and would likely increase the anonymity of the process. Furthermore, a voting process in the event of a stalemate can be faster, and (perhaps) more complex voting methods could be considered.

Transfer of the process to personal computers would also allow for the meeting to take place over multiple locations (i.e., each person in his or her own office or in different cities) and over a greater period of time (i.e. participants could log into the system at their convenience to enter votes and responses).

---

[35] Justification is not required, in order to prevent participants from entering values just above or below thresholds to avoid having to write a justification.

3.4.3. Capturing Uncertainty in Judgments

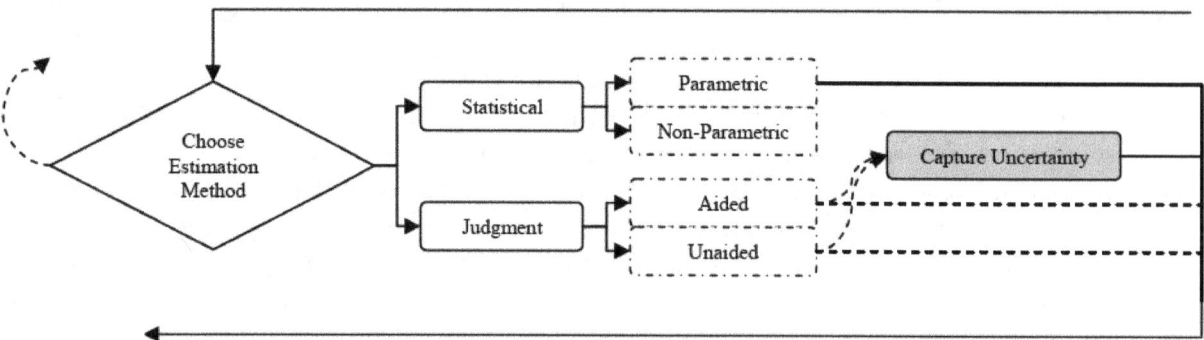

OMB Circulars A-94 and A-4 both emphasize the importance of conveying to decision makers the uncertainty surrounding the data that are employed in regulatory analyses.

> By assessing the sources of uncertainty and the way in which benefit and cost estimates may be affected under plausible assumptions, you can shape your analysis to inform decision makers and the public about the effects and the uncertainties of alternative regulatory actions.[36]

While the use of Monte Carlo methods is suggested, this requires that there be sufficient data. The triangular distribution can also be used to present information on the uncertainty surrounding a point estimate. It is commonly employed as a "rough model in the absence of data."[37] This approach is the simplest way to account for a range of uncertainty while representing an upper and lower bound as well as a mid-point describing the most likely value and when graphed out, looks like a triangle, as seen in

Figure 4. Note that an assumption embedded in this distributional form is that there in no chance, however small, that the parameter of interest takes on values outside the range (a, b). As a quasi-statistical technique, some summary and distributional information can be gleaned from it.

The mean value can be calculated as:

$$\mu = \frac{a+b+c}{3}$$

---

[36] See, Treatment of Uncertainty, Circular A-4, Office of Management and Budget.
[37] See, Averill Law and W. David Kelton, Simulation Modelling and Analysis, McGraw Hill, 1982, p. 167-168.

and the variance is:

$$\sigma^2 = \frac{a^2 + b^2 + c^2 - ab - ac - bc}{18}.$$

Creating these distributions can be done as part of an aided or unaided judgment method. Rather than ask experts for a single point estimate of the expected impact of a regulation on port processes and characteristics, experts can be asked for high, low, and most likely effects.

Now, the regulatory assessment can carry along information about how likely each value is within the range. With this information, sensitivity testing is able to be performed and the results are likely to be more robust.

Figure 4: The Triangular Distribution

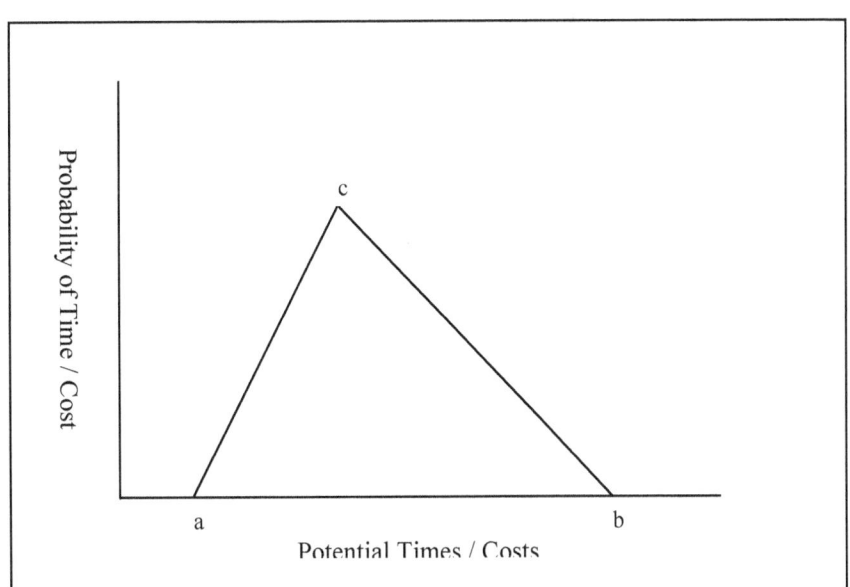

3.5. Calculate Overall Changes in Port Attributes

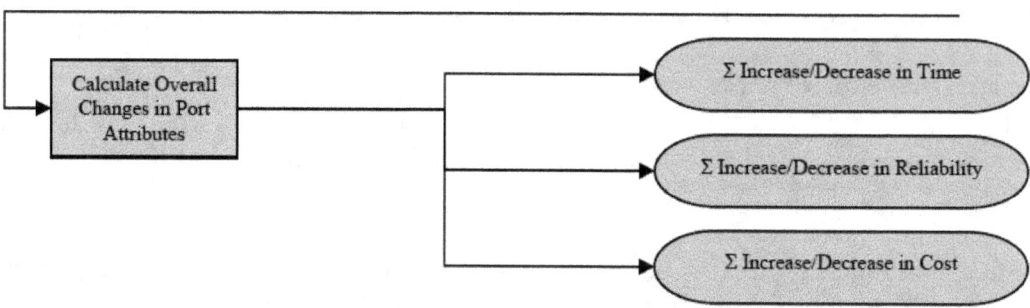

Once estimates have been made that support an understanding of the changes in port characteristics and processes that will accompany a new regulation, the effect of these changes on port attributes must be estimated. This requires empirical estimates of the sensitivity of container processing costs and times to changes in ports' physical characteristics or container-handling processes. These estimates can be drawn from a variety of sources including simulation studies, statistical estimates, or expert judgment.

The process also relies on empirical estimates of the sensitivity of demand for containerized cargo moving between the U.S. and its trading partners to changes in port costs and processing times. For regulations likely to have differential impacts on U.S. ports, the process may also require port-level estimates of the sensitivity of trade volumes to attributes of individual ports and their competitors. Again, these parameters may be obtainable from a variety of sources, but care and judgment will be required to adapt and employ them in the process described here. This discussion will continue using the statistical method outlined in Section 3.4.1.

Table 5 reports elasticities of port attributes that affect the demand for port services with respect to the port productivity measure used in Table 3. These attributes include container processing cost, container processing or dwell time, and the variance in processing time, a measure of reliability. Variation in container processing *costs* resulting from changes in port productivity is assumed to be reflected fully in corresponding changes in port *charges* for container movements.

Table 5: Elasticities of Port Service Attributes with Respect to Port Productivity

Port Name	State	U.S. Region	Elasticity of Port Attribute with Respect to Productivity:		
			Average Container Processing Cost	Average Container Processing Time	Reliability[38]
			($/container)	(days)	(days)
Baltimore	MD	Northeast	-0.68	-1.00	-0.50
Boston	MA	Northeast	-0.56	-1.00	-0.50
Charleston	SC	Southeast	-0.66	-1.00	-0.50
Galveston	TX	Gulf	-0.46	-1.00	-0.50
Houston	TX	Gulf	-0.60	-1.00	-0.50
Hampton Roads	VA	Southeast	-0.55	-1.00	-0.50
Jacksonville	FL	Southeast	-0.65	-1.00	-0.50
Los Angeles	CA	West	-0.59	-1.00	-0.50
Long Beach	CA	West	-0.56	-1.00	-0.50
Miami	FL	Southeast	-0.83	-1.00	-0.50
New Orleans	LA	Gulf	-0.68	-1.00	-0.50
New York/New Jersey	NY,NJ	Northeast	-0.75	-1.00	-0.50
Oakland	CA	West	-0.37	-1.00	-0.50
Port Everglades	FL	Gulf	-0.81	-1.00	-0.50
Philadelphia	PA	Northeast	-0.67	-1.00	-0.50
Portland	OR	West	-0.41	-1.00	-0.50
Savannah	GA	Southeast	-0.63	-1.00	-0.50
Seattle	WA	West	-0.95	-1.00	-0.50
San Francisco	CA	West	-0.06	-1.00	-0.50
Tacoma	WA	West	-0.97	-1.00	-0.50
Wilmington	DE	Northeast	-1.10	-1.00	-0.50
Wilmington	NC	Southeast	-0.65	-1.00	-0.50

The elasticities of container processing costs with respect to port productivity reported in Table 5 are derived from Blonigen and Wilson's econometric estimates of the components of total shipping charges for foreign-originating and destined cargo that represent charges levied by individual U.S. ports. The Blonigen-Wilson coefficient estimates are first converted to elasticities of total shipping charges with respect to

---

[38] Variance of container processing time about average.

changes in U.S. port efficiency or productivity. These parameters are then adjusted to the values reported in Table 5 using the estimated fraction of total shipping charges represented by U.S. port fees.[39]

As the elasticity of –1.0 shown in the table for all ports indicates, processing or dwell time is assumed to vary directly but inversely with a port's container-handling productivity. This is simply because port productivity is measured by container volume processed, and changes in processing time per container are inversely related to variation in container throughput. In the absence of any published empirical estimates of its relationship to port efficiency, changes in the variance of processing time are assumed to be only half as large as changes in average container dwell time.

Table 6 shows the changes in demand attributes for the Port of Seattle that are estimated to result from the hypothetical limitation on container stacking heights. These are derived by first multiplying the changes in port characteristics assumed to result from the regulation, shown previously in Table 4, by the elasticities of port productivity with respect to changes in port characteristics reported in Table 3. Summing the results of these calculations results in an estimated total reduction in productivity of 1.2% for the Port of Seattle, as a consequence of the changes in its characteristics required to comply with the hypothetical regulation.

The elasticities shown in Table 5 are then used to convert this estimated reduction in port productivity to changes in average container processing cost (and thus container-handling fees), dwell time, and its variance for the Port of Seattle. As Table 6 shows, the hypothetical regulation on stacking height is projected increase each of these attributes for Seattle. The modestness of these projected increases partly reflects the relatively limited impacts the hypothetical regulation on port characteristics, although it mainly reflects the small magnitudes of the elasticities of port productivity with respect to these characteristics.

---

[39] If port charges for container handling represent a fraction α of total shipping charges for a container, and the elasticity of total shipping charges with respect to port productivity is ε, then the elasticity of container-handling charges with respect to port productivity equals ε/α.

Table 6: Changes in Port Service Attributes Resulting from Sample Regulation

Port Name	State	U.S. Region	Percent Changes in Port Attributes:		
			Processing Cost	Processing Time	Reliability
Baltimore	MD	Northeast			
Boston	MA	Northeast			
Charleston	SC	Southeast			
Galveston	TX	Gulf			
Houston	TX	Gulf			
Hampton Roads	VA	Southeast			
Jacksonville	FL	Southeast			
Los Angeles	CA	West			
Long Beach	CA	West			
Miami	FL	Southeast			
New Orleans	LA	Gulf			
New York/New Jersey	NY,NJ	Northeast			
Oakland	CA	West			
Port Everglades	FL	Gulf			
Philadelphia	PA	Northeast			
Portland	OR	West			
Savannah	GA	Southeast			
Seattle	WA	West	1.3%	1.3%	0.7%
San Francisco	CA	West			
Tacoma	WA	West			
Wilmington	DE	Northeast			
Wilmington	NC	Southeast			

3.6. Trade Impacts

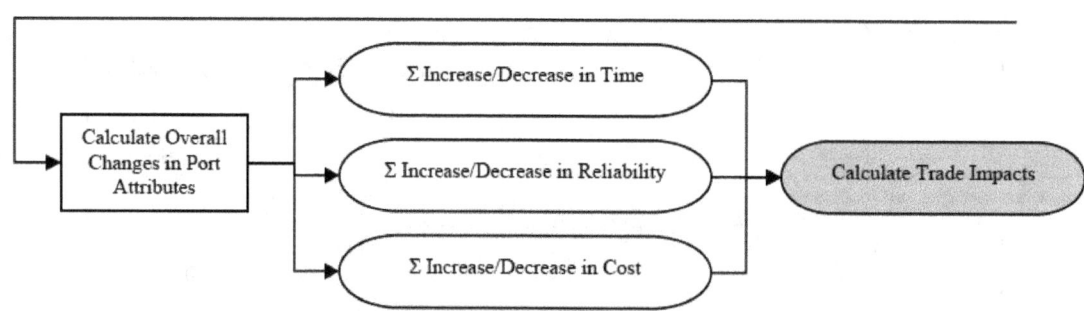

Table 7 combines the estimated elasticities of port attributes with respect to productivity reported in Table 5 with the Blonigen-Wilson estimates of the elasticity of container shipping volume through U.S. ports with respect to total shipping charges. This produces estimates of the sensitivity (elasticity) of demand for containerized shipments through U.S. ports to changes in each port attribute. Variation in container dwell time is converted to an equivalent change in port tariffs using the average daily inventory value of container cargo.

As Table 7 illustrates, the variation in ports' elasticities of container processing costs with respect to productivity shown previously in Table 5 is reflected in similar variation in the elasticities of demand for container shipping through individual ports. (Again, increases in average container processing costs are assumed to be fully recouped by ports through increases in the charges and fees they levy for various aspects of container handling and processing.) The elasticities of demand for container shipping with respect to container processing time and reliability shown in Table 7 are provisionally assumed to be identical among U.S. ports, pending the identification or development of port-specific values for these parameters.

Finally, Table 8 uses the elasticities of container shipping demand from Table 7 to anticipate the effects of the regulation on overall container shipping activity at the Port of Seattle. Because the regulation is estimated to increase container tariffs, dwell times, and dwell time variance, it is expected to lead to a decline in demand for containerized cargo shipping through the sample port (Seattle). As Table 8 shows, each of the changes in port attributes is expected to lead to only a slight reduction in shipping demand, but their combined effect is a more significant reduction in demand, because the change in each attribute affects demand in the same direction.[40] In contrast, other regulations might affect port, container cargo, or vessel characteristics so as to reduce container processing time (or its variance), while simultaneously increasing average processing cost. In that

---

[40] The combined effect of the changes in demand from the changes in the three attributes is not additive, because these changes are expressed in percentage rather than in absolute terms. As this example illustrates, however, the separate effects of the percentage changes in the attributes are approximately additive when each of them is small.

case, the effects of such a change on shipping demand at ports affected by such a regulation would partly or completely offset each other.

Table 7: Elasticities of Port Demand with Respect to Port Service Attributes

| Port Name | State | U.S. Region | Elasticity of Port Demand with Respect to Service Attribute: | | |
| | | | Average Container Processing Cost | Average Container Processing Time | Reliability |
			($/container)	(days)	(days)
Baltimore	MD	Northeast	-0.22	-0.32	-0.16
Boston	MA	Northeast	-0.18	-0.32	-0.16
Charleston	SC	Southeast	-0.21	-0.32	-0.16
Galveston	TX	Gulf	-0.15	-0.32	-0.16
Houston	TX	Gulf	-0.19	-0.32	-0.16
Hampton Roads	VA	Southeast	-0.18	-0.32	-0.16
Jacksonville	FL	Southeast	-0.21	-0.32	-0.16
Los Angeles	CA	West	-0.19	-0.32	-0.16
Long Beach	CA	West	-0.18	-0.32	-0.16
Miami	FL	Southeast	-0.27	-0.32	-0.16
New Orleans	LA	Gulf	-0.22	-0.32	-0.16
New York/New Jersey	NY,NJ	Northeast	-0.24	-0.32	-0.16
Oakland	CA	West	-0.12	-0.32	-0.16
Port Everglades	FL	Gulf	-0.26	-0.32	-0.16
Philadelphia	PA	Northeast	-0.22	-0.32	-0.16
Portland	OR	West	-0.13	-0.32	-0.16
Savannah	GA	Southeast	-0.20	-0.32	-0.16
Seattle	WA	West	-0.30	-0.32	-0.16
San Francisco	CA	West	-0.02	-0.32	-0.16
Tacoma	WA	West	-0.31	-0.32	-0.16
Wilmington	DE	Northeast	-0.35	-0.32	-0.16
Wilmington	NC	Southeast	-0.21	-0.32	-0.16

Table 8: Changes in Port Demand Resulting from Sample Regulation

Port Name	State	U.S. Region	Percent Change in Port Demand Due to Change in Attribute:			
			Processing Cost	Processing Time	Reliability	All Attributes
Baltimore	MD	Northeast				
Boston	MA	Northeast				
Charleston	SC	Southeast				
Galveston	TX	Gulf				
Houston	TX	Gulf				
Hampton Roads	VA	Southeast				
Jacksonville	FL	Southeast				
Los Angeles	CA	West				
Long Beach	CA	West				
Miami	FL	Southeast				
New Orleans	LA	Gulf				
New York/New Jersey	NY,NJ	Northeast				
Oakland	CA	West				
Port Everglades	FL	Gulf				
Philadelphia	PA	Northeast				
Portland	OR	West				
Savannah	GA	Southeast				
Seattle	WA	West	-0.4%	-0.4%	-0.1%	-0.9%
San Francisco	CA	West				
Tacoma	WA	West				
Wilmington	DE	Northeast				
Wilmington	NC	Southeast				

It is important to note that the hypothetical effect of the stacking height regulation on container shipping demand via the Port of Seattle shown in Table 8 assumes that this regulation would affect all U.S. container ports uniformly. This is because the elasticities of container shipping demand at individual ports shown previously in Table 7 reflect the estimated elasticities of aggregate U.S. container trade with respect to container fees (costs), processing time, and the reliability of processing time. Since changes in aggregate U.S. trade in containerized cargo are assumed to be distributed among ports in approximate proportion to their initial volumes of containerized cargo, these changes do not result in any reallocation of container shipping demand among U.S. ports.

Comparable elasticities of container shipping demand at any *single* port with respect to changes in these attributes would be much larger than those shown in Table 7, since they would incorporate potentially significant reallocations of container shipping demand to or from each individual port when only its own attributes changed.[41] Analyzing the effects of changes in the port regulatory environment that are expected to have different effects on the port, cargo, or vessel characteristics of specific individual ports would require estimates of the elasticities of individual ports' shares of total U.S. containerized cargo volume with respect to port-specific attribute values. This is in addition to the estimates of aggregate U.S. container shipping demand used in this sample analysis.

---

[41] The elasticity of demand for containerized cargo shipping via any single U.S. port with respect to one of the attributes (container charges, dwell time, or reliability) of *that* port is the sum of (1) the elasticity of total container shipping demand at all U.S. ports with respect to a uniform change in that attribute at *all* ports, plus (2) the elasticity of that port's *share* of total U.S. container shipping demand with respect to its own value of the attribute. As long as component (2) is non-zero, the magnitude of this sum will be larger than the magnitude of component (1).

4. SUMMARY AND RECOMMENDATIONS

4.1. The Analytic Framework

This report has developed a detailed framework to support transparent and consistent evaluation of the potential impacts of changes in the port regulatory environment proposed by the U.S. Coast Guard. These impacts are initiated by the effects of new regulations or extensions of existing regulations on the physical characteristics of container ports, on ports' "production functions" for container-handling operations, and on container vessels and their cargo.

The proposed framework translates these changes into estimated impacts on the productivity or efficiency of ports' container-handling operations, and subsequently into projected changes in processing costs, container dwell times at ports, and reliability of container dwell times. Finally, it projects the resulting changes in demand for containerized cargo shipments through U.S. ports in response to regulation-induced changes in port tariffs, dwell times, and the variability of those dwell times.

The report also demonstrates the utility and applicability of this proposed framework using a specific example of a regulation limiting container stacking heights in ports' staging and storage areas. Such a regulation would be expected to reduce container throughput capacity at individual container terminals and ports, while also requiring ports to dedicate additional land area to container staging and temporary storage.

Although this example is useful in itself to demonstrate the mechanics of the regulatory assessment process, it also provides parameters that are likely to be useful in assessing the potential effects of future regulations proposed by the Coast Guard. These include measures of the sensitivity of port productivity to changes in port and container vessel characteristics, the impacts of productivity changes on ports' container processing times and costs, and the sensitivity of demand for containerized cargo shipping via U.S. ports.

4.2. Value of the Analytic Framework

This analysis has synthesized the fragmented literature on ports using a framework that relates characteristics of container ports, their production processes, and vessels serving them to port attributes that affect shipping demand, and finally to containerized cargo shipments between U.S. ports and trading partners. Virtually all previous studies of ports have analyzed some limited aspect of this overarching framework, focused on the institutional characteristics of ports while ignoring their regulatory environment, or represented their production processes using abstract mathematical production and cost functions.

As a result, their usefulness for tracing the effect of regulatory changes through to changes in demand attributes and trade flows, or for drawing conclusions about the reaction of port demand attributes to changes in the regulatory environment that can be generalized across U.S. ports is very limited. In contrast, the framework developed here synthesizes previous research into a process for tracing the potential consequences of regulations on port characteristics and activity through to the outcomes that determine their ultimate impact on their regional economies and U.S. aggregate trade flows.

The process outlined above relies heavily on empirical estimates of critical parameters that determine these outcomes obtained from the limited number of published econometric studies of port productivity and costs. However, these estimates are used primarily to illustrate the regulatory assessment process and to "calibrate" the framework provisionally. They can be replaced with values derived from more reliable econometric analyses, port simulation studies, or expert-based methods, and estimates drawn from different sources can readily be mixed.

For example, simulation models would appear to be the most logical source for estimating the effect of changes in changes in ports' production processes required to comply with security-related regulations on their labor and capital utilization or on different stages of container-handling operations. In contrast, statistical analysis of port production functions should be an ideal resource for estimating the consequences of restrictions on ports' use of inputs for costs and container dwell times. Econometric models of the determinants of cargo types and trade volumes flowing through competing U.S. gateway ports seem to be the most logical source for estimating elasticities of demand for port services with respect to changing tariffs and dwell times. The important point is that different sources are likely to be suited for developing the various parameter values required to calibrate the regulatory assessment framework and support its use for evaluating regulations proposed by the Coast Guard.

4.3. Recommendations for Further Work

Additional research on container ports that relates operationally meaningful port characteristics to efficiency or productivity in their container-handling operations could improve the reliability of regulatory impact assessments for ports. Past studies have relied on easily observable or measurable characteristics – such as quay length or dock area – as proxies or substitutes for underlying variables that actually influence productivity.

More importantly, the relationship of variables that are likely to be affected by regulations on port configuration or operations to ports' container-handling productivity needs to be better understood and documented in order to support improved regulatory assessment capabilities. At the same time, increasing the range of port, vessel, and cargo characteristics that affect port operations – and thus productivity – and that are themselves likely to be altered in response to security-related regulations on port activity should also be a priority of future research.

This analysis also assumed that the effect of regulations on port productivity was likely to be uniform. Research that investigates variation in the response of individual port efficiency to changes in their physical or operational characteristics would support differentiation among ports' expected responses to uniform nationwide regulations on port activity.

For example, differences among characteristics such as labor intensity or utilization of specific capital equipment might be expected to cause their productivity levels to respond differently to new regulatory requirements for security measures such as container inspection. Knowledge of these differences would be useful for projecting variation in how proposed regulations are likely to change container tariffs or dwell times at different ports, and how such regulations might redistribute containerized trade flows as a consequence of their differential effects on specific ports' demand attributes.

In short, a theory that unifies port configuration, operations, productivity, and resource use has not yet been developed. Its absence forces regulatory assessment to merge previous analyses of isolated aspects of the relationship among these concepts into a coherent framework.

Future research that clarifies the critical variables likely to be affected by regulations on port inputs or operations, and traces the impacts of changes in those measures through the causal chain represented in the analytic framework presented in this study, is likely to be particularly useful for improving the reliability of regulatory assessment. Finally, research that identifies observable port characteristics that are likely to cause the productivity and demand impacts of changes in the regulatory environment to vary among individual ports will also improve the specificity and reliability of future regulatory assessments.

APPENDIX A: LIST OF REVIEWED LITERATURE

American Association of Port Authorities, *Port Security Fees*, 2006, Available at: http://www.aapa-ports.org/Industry?&navItemNumber=494, Last Accessed: Feb 16, 2007.

Abstract:
As requested by the Executive Committee the AAPA staff is compiling a record of fees or surcharges assessed by port authorities of North America to recover security-related costs.

Armbruster, Bill, "Braking Port Bottlenecks: Shipper Advocate Calls for Better Use of Existing Port Facilities to Speed Cargo, Blames Railroads for Delays", *Traffic World*, June 19, 2006.

Abstract:
Shippers, carriers, ports, and terminal operators worried about bottlenecks and other ailments should pluck some low-hanging fruit to get at least some temporary relief. That's the prescription of Robin Lainer, executive director of the Waterfront Coalition, a shipper advocacy group.

Beck, Bill, "Ports prepare for the new millennium," *Easton*, Vol. 34:8, Aug 1999. p. 46-53.

Abstract:
The contemporary port isn't just loading and unloading cargo; it's dealing with real-world issues including land use, pollution, competition, and regulation.

Berman, Jeff, "PierPASS OffPeak program making strides with Ports of Los Angeles and Long Beach drivers," *Logistics Management*, Feb 2, 2007.

Abstract:
An increased number of trips truckers make per shift, a traffic reduction at the Ports of Los Angeles and Long Beach, and a more flexible work schedule were some of the benefits of PierPASS' Offpeak program cited by truck drivers in an opinion survey.

Blonigen, Bruce A. and Wesley W. Wilson, *International Trade, Transportation Networks, and Port Choice,* 2007 American Economic Association Conference, available at: http://www.aeaweb.org/annual_mtg_papers/2007/conference_papers.php, last accessed: March 28, 2007, May 2006.

Abstract:
As the clearinghouses for a major portion of the world's rapidly increasing international trade flows, ocean ports and the efficiency with which they process cargo have become an ever more important topic. Yet, there exist very little data that allows one to compare port efficiency measures of any kind across ports and, especially, over time. This paper provides a new statistical method of uncovering port efficiency measures using U.S. Census data on imports into U.S. ports. Unlike previous measures, this study's methodology can provide such estimates for a much broader sample of countries and years with little cost. Thus, such data can be used by future researchers to examine a myriad of new issues, including the evolution of port efficiencies over time and its effects on international trade flows and country-level growth.

Blonigen, Bruce A. and Wesley W. Wilson, *Port Efficiency and Trade Flows,* Institute for Water Resources, U.S. Army Corps of Engineers, IWR Report 06-NETS-R-11, Arlington, Virginia, United States, November 2006.

Abstract:
Rapid increases in international trade have led to congestion in many of the worlds' ports and have raised concern over the ability of transportation networks to handle the increased volumes. Increased volumes and the resulting congestion may impact trade flow patterns by affecting choices of importers and exporters. Trade flow patterns are most certainly determined by a wide variety of factors that include the internal (intra-country) and external (inter-country) transport costs, as well as the costs of interchange (port costs). Yet, there is little evidence that documents each of these factors in the determination of trade flow patterns. As any of these factors become relatively more or less congested, there may be significant impacts not only on the network paths chosen, but also on the volume of activity. This paper develops a model of port choice and trading volumes and then estimates the impact of ocean transport rates, efficiency of U.S. ocean ports, and internal transport systems on port choice and trade volume over a sample trade flows between over 150 foreign countries and the top U.S. ports for the period from 1991 through 2003. Our estimates provide strong evidence for the importance of economic factors in port choices. Distance and transport prices are very significant factors with quite elastic responses by shipments well above one in absolute magnitude. Unlike previous studies, this paper's analysis finds a significant role for an individual's port efficiency in determining its share of activity, with estimates ranging from 0.8 to 2.0 depending on the empirical specification used.

Blonigen, Bruce A. and Wesley W. Wilson, *New Measures of Port Efficiency Using International Trade Data*, National Bureau of Economic Research, Working Paper 12052, Available at: http://www.nber.org/papers/w12052, February, 2006.

Abstract:
While there are many applications of this method and the resulting port efficiency measures, we focus on using our measures to examine the relationship between port efficiency and international trade flows in a standard gravity-trade specification. Clark et al. (2004) and Wilson et al. (2004) estimate this relationship using survey measures of port efficiency drawn from the Global Competitiveness Report. A potential drawback of these studies is that the survey measures are for only a point in time and may proxy other unobserved country characteristics. In contrast, our port efficiency measures are time-varying, allowing controls for unobserved country-level heterogeneity in trade flows. We find that port efficiency is quite important in explaining trade flows between countries with a statistically-significant elasticity of 0.4 after controlling for unobserved country-level heterogeneity. While significant, this is much lower than the elasticity we estimate when excluding country-level fixed effects; this suggests that previous studies may be overstating the impact of port efficiency on trade. The rest of the paper proceeds as follows. After briefly reviewing related previous literature in the next section, we provide details of our statistical methodology to uncover U.S. and foreign port efficiency in section 3. Section 4 , describes our data, while section 5 provides the papers statistical results new efficiency rankings of U.S. and foreign ports, as well as gravity model estimates of the effect of port efficiency on international trade flows.

Bonney, Joseph, "On Schedules," *Journal of Commerce*, June 5, 2006.

Abstract:
Company press releases often contain well-worn phrases that we try to avoid. One is "state of the art," a tired cliché, that can mean whatever anyone wants it to mean. Another is "fixed-day" port calls. Despite carriers' best efforts, most port calls aren't fixed-day. As Peter Leach points out on Page 10 in this week's magazine, a study in a new quarterly publication by Drewry Shipping Consultants has quantified the gap between the schedules and arrival dates of 63 ocean container lines.

Charles River Associates Incorporated, *Proposed Alaska-Canada Rail Link: A Review of Potential Benefits*, Yukon Government Department of Economic Development, available at:http://www.economicdevelopment.gov.yk.ca/documents/AlasCanRailLinkExecSumm.pdf, last accessed: March 28, 2007, March, 2005.

Abstract:
Effectively developing the Alaska-Canada Rail Link will require cooperation of both the U.S. and Canadian governments as well as the governments of Alaska, the Yukon, and British Columbia. Government involvement will address two essential functions related to this project's development. First, government will ensure that external costs and benefits not captured in market demands and prices are taken into account in developing the corridor. Second, government will reduce transaction costs that might hinder the private development of the corridor by disseminating information, removing bureaucratic barriers, and coordinating diverse interests.
It is reasonable for the Government to devote financial support to a detailed feasibility study that will shape this project's definition, detail the business case, and facilitate the efforts of the private sector. This study would be a valuable first step towards addressing coordination problems. It would allow interested parties to begin their planning processes based on a common base of well-founded analysis. By sponsoring such a study, governments will encourage private investors to take a hard look at this opportunity. Investors will more readily be able to make informed decisions regarding the true costs and benefits associated with the future development of the Alaska-Canada Rail Link. We believe the U.S. and Canadian governments will be able to jointly design a comprehensive feasibility study to meet those objectives.

Clark, Ximena, David Dollar, and Alejandro Micco, "Maritime Transport Costs and Port Efficiency," Presented at LACEA, Montevideo, Uruguay, 2001, available at http://www.lacea.org/meeting2001/Clark.pdf.

Abstract:
Recent literature has emphasized the importance of transport costs and infrastructure in explaining trade, access to markets, and increases in per capita income. For most Latin American countries, transport costs are a greater barrier to U.S. markets than import tariffs. We investigate the determinants of shipping costs to the U.S. with a large database of more than 300,000 observations per year on shipments of products at the six-digit HS level from different ports around the world. Distance and containerization matter. In addition, we find that efficiency of ports is an important determinant of shipping costs. Improving port efficiency from the 25th to the 75th percentile reduces shipping costs by 12 percent. (Bad ports are equivalent to being 60% farther away from markets for the average country.) Inefficient ports also increase handling costs, which are one of the components of shipping costs. Finally, we try to explain variations in port efficiency and find that they are linked to excessive regulation, the prevalence of organized crime, and the general condition of the country's infrastructure.

Clark, Ximena, David Dollar, and Alejandro Micco, *Port Efficiency, Maritime Transport Costs and Bilateral Trade*, National Bureau of Economic Research, Working Paper 10353, Available at: http://www.nber.org/papers/w10353, February, 2006.

Abstract:
Recent literature has emphasized the importance of transport costs and infrastructure in explaining trade, access to markets, and increases in per capita income. For most Latin American countries, transport costs are a greater barrier to U.S. markets than import tariffs. We investigate the determinants of shipping costs to the U.S. with a large database of more than 300,000 observations per year on shipments of products aggregated at six-digit HS level from different ports around the world. Distance, volumes and product characteristics matter. In addition, we find that ports efficiency is an important determinant of shipping costs. Improving port efficiency from the 25th to the 75th percentile reduces shipping costs by 12 percent. (Bad ports are equivalent to being 60% farther away from markets for the average country.) Inefficient ports also increase handling costs, which are one of the components of shipping costs. Reductions in country inefficiencies associated to transport costs from the 25th to 75th percentiles imply an increase in bilateral trade of around 25 percent. Finally, we try to explain variations in port efficiency and find that they are linked to excessive regulation, the prevalence of organized crime, and the general condition of the country's infrastructure.

Cullinane, Kevin, Teng-Fei Wang, Dong-Wook Song, and Ping Ji, "The technical efficiency of container ports: Comparing data envelopment analysis and stochastic frontier analysis", *Transportation Research Part A*, 2006, p. 354-374.

Abstract:
The efficiency of the container port industry has been variously studied utilizing either Data Envelopment Analysis (DEA) or Stochastic Frontier Analysis (SFA). Given the strengths and weaknesses associated with these two approaches, the efficiency estimates and scale properties derived from these analyses are not always convincing. This paper applies both approaches to the same set of container port data for the world s largest container ports and compares the results obtained. A high degree of correlation is found between the efficiency estimates derived from all the models applied, suggesting that results are relatively robust to the DEA models applied or the distributional assumptions under SFA. High levels of technical efficiency are associated with scale, greater private-sector participation and with trans-shipment as opposed to gateway ports. In analyzing the implications of the results for management and policy makers, a number of shortcomings of applying a cross-sectional approach to an industry characterized by significant, lumpy and risky investments are identified and the potential benefits of a dynamic analysis, based on panel data, are enumerated.

Customs and Border Patrol, *Summary of Rule by Mode,* Trade Act of 2002- Advance Electronic Information, available at: http://www.cbp.gov/xp/cgov/import/communications_to_trade/advance_info/, last accessed: March 28, 2007, 2002.

Daniels, Wade, Port delays lead to boost in costlier air cargo shipments - Long Beach and Los Angeles, CA, *Los Angeles Business Journal,* Nov 17, 1997.

Abstract:
Fearful that congestion at the seaports of Long Beach and Los Angeles may lead to disastrous delays in their product deliveries, some area businesses have begun importing by air.

Dundovic, Čedomir, and Zdenka Zenzerovic, "An Optimal Capacity Planning Model for General Cargo Seaport," *Traffic Planning,* Vol. 12: 5-6, 2000, p. 217-221.

Abstract:
In this paper the application of the queuing theory in optimal capacity planning for general cargo seaport is presented. The seaport as a queuing system is defined and thus, on the basis of the arrival and serviced number of ships in an observed time unit, the appropriate operating indicators of a port system are calculated. Using the model of total port costs, the number of berths and cranes on the berth can be determined whereby the optimal port system functioning is achieved

Edmonson, R.G., Help is on the Way, *Journal of Commerce,* October 2, 2006.

Abstract:
It could be that non-vessel-operating common carriers are the canaries in the coal mine when it comes to detecting early signs of port congestion. NVOs' consolidated containers get held for inspection more frequently than full loads, even though Customs and Border Protection may be interested in just one shipper's goods among several in the box. "NVOCCs are much more susceptible to exams, given the variety of cargo in the container. The national average for inspections is 5 percent. We're probably 80 percent of that 5 percent," said Joe Muniere, chairman of the NVO committee for the National Customs Brokers and Forwarders Association of America. Cargo delays mean shippers pay more, because terminals don't stop the clock on demurrage charges for a Customs hold.

Gordon, Peter, James E Moore, II, Harry W. Richardson, and Qisheng Pan, "The Economic Impact of a Terrorist Attack on the Twin Ports of Los Angeles-Long Beach", Create Report Number 05-012, available at: http://www.usc.edu/dept/create/research/reports.htm, last accessed: March 28, 2007, May, 2005.

Abstract:
The Los Angeles metropolitan region is a prime target for a terrorist attack. There are many specific targets: the Los Angeles International Airport (LAX), downtown high-rises, its theme parks, its freeways, and its ports, among many others. We have developed a spatially disaggregated economic impact model that can evaluate all of these and any other plausible attacks. In this paper, we estimate the economic impacts of an attack on the Los Angeles-Long Beach Twin Ports.

Graham, D. Wesley, C. Richard Cassady, Royce O. Bowden, and Stephen A. LeMay, "Modeling Intermodal Transportation Systems: Establishing a Common Language", available at: http://www.ise.msstate.edu/ncit/RESEARCH.html, last accessed: March 28, 2007.

Abstract:
While the ultimate goal of defining a language that is broadly accepted by analysts and the intermodal industry will be difficult to achieve, the terminology base presented in this paper covers a majority of the elements and activity involved in the operation of intermodal transportation systems and provides a foundation for building models of such systems. Undoubtedly, future research will reveal additional terminology and refinements to facilitate the modeling and analysis of intermodal systems. However, an efficient national intermodal transportation system will not be realized unless real problems are defined, models of these problems are constructed, and analysis of model outputs are used to identify and implement the most efficient solutions. The terminology base presented in this paper establishes a common language from which analysts can begin this important endeavor.

Grigalunas, Thomas A., Meifeng Luo and Bong Min Jung, *Comprehensive Framework for Sustainable Container Ports Development of US East Coast in the 21st Century: Year Two*, University of Rhode Island Transportation Center, URITC Project Number 536140, DOT Number URITC FY00-10, August 2002.

Abstract:
Building upon the conceptual framework developed during our year one research, a container port and multimodal transportation demand simulation model is applied. The model selects the least-cost (vessel-portrail- truck) route from sources to markets, where costs are defined as total general costs--costs for using each transportation facility plus interest on the value of investment in containerized goods. The database in the model includes all state and federal highways, the Class I rail system, and oceangoing and near shore shipping routes. For the US, the analysis is at the state level (at the county level for the Northeast). Outside the US, analysis is at the continent level, except for Asia, which is divided into East and West Asia (Singapore and West). Best available data are used as input for economic parameters. Key results show (1) estimated annual demand for 14 major US coastal ports for 1999, (2) the transportation routes for different markets, sources, and cargo values, (3) market areas (the "extent of the market") served by major ports, and (4) interport demand changes due to hypothetical fee changes at selected ports. Then, the model is used to illustrate estimation of (4) the initial demand for a hypothetical new port and (5) the importance of availability of double -stack train rail access and competition from other ports for the hypothetical port. These results then were used, along with other information, to estimate the financial feasibility and risk for the hypothetical port. Limitations, qualifications and refinements and extensions are noted.

Grigalunas, Thomas A., Meifeng Luo, Simona Trandafir, Christopher Anderson, and Suk Jae Kwon, *Issues in Container Transportation in the Northeast: Background, Framework, Illustrative Results and Future Directions,* University of Rhode Island Transportation Center, URITC Project Number 536185, DOT Number URITC FY02-11, December 2004.

Abstract:
An integrated framework for addressing container transportation issues in the Northeast US is developed and illustrated. The framework involves the extension of a spatial-economic coastal container port and related multimodal demand simulation model to include a hub and spoke feeder system, with the Port of New York and New Jersey (PNYNJ) as the hub. When applied, the extended model would incorporate the introduction of barges for short-haul of containers and enhanced rail to distribute containers from the PNYNJ to distribution centers throughout the Northeast, by that reducing truck travel or regional roads and bridges. Potential environmental benefits from reduced truck traffic, such as air emissions, road wear and tear, and fewer accidents, may result. Extensions of the model to include shadow prices for such external effects are described and illustrated using, as a case study, potential benefits from reduced emissions of NOx from a hypothetical feeder facility on Narragansett Bay. Inter-port competition also is described and estimates of cross demand effects for other coastal ports are simulated. Possible strategic behavior by a hub port against potential competitors using an entrance deterrent model is presented.

Grigalunas, Thomas A., Young-Tae Chang, and Meifeng Luo, "Containerport Investment Appraisal and Risk Analysis: Illustrative Case Study", *Transportation Research Record*, Number 1782, Paper Number 02-3840, 2002.

Abstract:
There are considerable economic and political pressures to expand existing and develop new containerports to accommodate the increasing trade of containerized cargoes carried on ever-larger vessels. However, port development involves a major investment and poses many financial, economic, and environmental risks. The major sources of financial risk facing prospective terminal operators are reviewed and methods to identify the overall financial risk and importance of individual sources of risk are illustrated. Methods used focus on net present value and the use of extensive sensitivity analyses as well as the use of the more formal Monte Carlo analysis. A dynamic discrete-event model is also employed to assess the internal consistency and feasibility of a developer's port plans and projected operations. Generalized data from previous early engineering–economic studies of a proposed port at Quonset Point, on Narragansett Bay, Rhode Island, are employed to illustrate the use of these methods. Four specific risks are considered: start-up volume of moves, growth rate of moves, costs, and efficiency of yard operations. Results suggest that the start-up volume and growth rate of moves are critical factors in the financial success of a proposed port. Results can be extended to more variables and refined when information on more current specific port plans becomes available.

Hackett, Ben, "Forecast for 2007: No congestion", *Journal of Commerce*, January 15, 2007.

Abstract:
The port and maritime industry appears to be fixated on the theme of congestion and high utilization, be it on sea or land. For the former, we can see that there is significant spare capacity, but that liner operators are managing it much better than in the past. They are removing capacity to maintain the illusion of full ships and the need for higher freight rates. This is a sound policy that helps maintain freight revenue and avoids the violent swings apparent in the past. The ports have a different issue. Port authorities, terminal operators, liner operators, railroads and labor are all joining in the mantra of port and inland congestion. Are we facing congestion, will we have congestion, or is this also an illusion to help gain investment dollars and increased charges?

Harrington, Lisa H., "Breaking Point: Ports Perform Under Pressure", *Inbound Logistics*, June 2006.

Abstract:
U.S container ports are busy trying to update aging infrastructure and ease congestion, while handling increased demand. Can the government and private sector help? What does the future hold?

Harrison, Robert, Miguel A. Figliozzi, and C. Michael Walton, Mega-Containerships and Mega-Containerports in the Gulf of Mexico: A Literature Review and Annotated Bibliography (See Chapter 6: Mega-Containership Impacts on Port Infrastructure), Center for Transportation Research, Bureau of Engineering Research at University of Texas at Austin, Research Project Number 0-1833, Report Number 1833-1, FHWA Report Number FHWA/TX-00/1833-1, May, 2000.

Abstract:
Container shipping plays a key role in international transshipments and is currently the system of choice for most global shippers handling non-bulk commodities. In the competitive maritime industry, steamship companies are looking for ways in which further economies can be achieved. One of the areas examined has been the maritime portion of the trip, wherein ship economies of scale can be obtained through the use of larger vessels. During the 1990s, technical constraints associated with very large or mega-containership designs were overcome, and the operation of such vessels (in the range of 4,500 to 7,000 TEUs) offered the promise of lower container shipment costs over the densest trade routes. This report represents the findings of a literature review largely undertaken during the period from August 1998 to June 1999. The report includes chapters on international trade and maritime economics, maritime industry, containerization, mega-containerships, and mega-containerport infrastructure, and concludes with recommendations concerning the deliverables required for Research Project 0-1833. An annotated bibliography containing material used in the report is given in the Appendix.

Haughey, James, "Shippers report negative impact from West Coast port backup," *Logistics Management*, December 2, 2004.

Abstract:
According to a Logistics Management survey conducted in late November, shippers are reporting enough of a negative impact from the West Coat port backups that they have made temporary changes in their shipping plans and have made, or are considering, long-term shipping changes to avoid more costly delays.

Heffron, Ronald E., *What Is Life-Cycle Management and What Can It Do for Me and My Port Structures?*, Proceedings of Ports '04: Port Development in the Changing World, available at: http://www.han-padron.com/papers.asp, last accessed: March 28, 2007, May 2004.

Abstract:
Life-cycle management (LCM) is a term familiar to many design engineers, but is understood by few. Some even dismiss it as the latest hollow buzzword with little practical value. Nothing could be further from the truth. In fact, LCM at its best represents a structured approach to asset planning, design, construction, and operation that maximizes functionality while minimizing life-cycle costs. This paper summarizes the recent work of the International Navigation Association (formerly known as PIANC) Working Group 42, of which the author is a U.S. Delegate. The LCM concept is generally in a primitive stage of implementation worldwide, with European nations somewhat ahead of their counterparts in other nations.
In practice, LCM applies to both new and existing structures throughout the four key life-cycle stages:
1. Planning and design
2. Construction
3. Operation and maintenance
4. Reuse or removal
With these four life-cycle stages in mind, LCM implementation focuses on the following performance parameters: a) serviceability, b) availability, c) durability, d) environmental compatibility, e) aesthetics, f) safety, g) constructability, h) inspectability, i) maintainability, j) upgradeability, k) reusability, l) replaceability, m) sustainability, and n) removability. Each of these performance parameters are described in this paper and examples are provided to illustrate the concept. Finally, the concept of whole life costing is introduced as a way to evaluate the parameters and achieve optimal design decisions.

Hoppin, David, "How Much Does Congestion Cost?" *Logistics Today*, September, 2006.

Abstract:
Bottlenecks and constraints on infrastructure can add costs that will scuttle any company's sourcing strategy.

Hsu, Chaug-Ing and Yu-Ping Hsieh, "Routing, ship size, and sailing frequency decision-making for a maritime hub-and-spoke container network," *Mathematical and Computer Modelling,* Vol. 45, 2007, p. 899-916.

Abstract:
This study formulates a two-objective model to determine the optimal liner routing, ship size, and sailing frequency for container carriers by minimizing shipping costs and inventory costs. First, shipping and inventory cost functions are formulated using an analytical method. Then, based on a trade-off between shipping costs and inventory costs, Pareto optimal solutions of the two objective model are determined. Not only can the optimal ship size and sailing frequency be determined for any route, but also the routing decision on whether to route containers through a hub or directly to their destination can be made in objective value space. Finally, the theoretical findings are applied to a case study, with highly reasonable results. The results show that the optimal routing, ship size, and sailing frequency with respect to each level of inventory costs and shipping costs can be determined using the proposed model. The optimal routing decision tends to be shipping the cargo through a hub as the hub charge is decreased or its efficiency improved. In addition, the proposed model not only provides a tool to analyze the trade-off between shipping costs and inventory costs, but it also provides flexibility on the decision-making for container carriers.

Huynh, Nathan N. and C. Michael Walton, *Methodologies for Reducing Truck Turn Time at Marine Container Terminals*, Southwest Region University Transportation Center, Texas Transportation Institute, Texas A&M University System and Center for Transportation Research, The University of Texas at Austin, Research Report 167830-1, US DOT Report Number SWUTC/05/167830-1, May 2005.

Abstract:
One of the prominent issues container terminal operators in the US are seeking to address is how to effectively reduce truck turn time. Historically, truck turn time has received very little attention from terminal operators because port congestion has never been a barrier to their operations. However, with the recent explosive growth in containerized trade, terminals are straining to accommodate the truck traffic that moves through them. The heavy intermodal truck traffic is not only causing problems for terminal operators but for the public as well. The emissions from idling trucks are a hazard to people working and living in and around the terminals. With containerized trade volume expected to double in the next ten years, the problems associated with port congestion could get worse if measures are not taken to address the source of the problems.

Terminals in some areas of the US are now required by state law to expedite the flow of trucks through their terminals. In California, any truck that idles for more than thirty minutes will result in a $250 fine to the terminal operator. This law has prompted terminal operators to look for ways to move trucks through their terminals faster, not just to avoid paying the fine, but also to lower the inland transportation cost of shipping a container via their terminals to remain competitive. This research investigates the two measures terminal operators are taking to reduce their terminals' truck turn time. The first measure is investing in additional yard cranes to facilitate the handling of containers. To this end, this research seeks to assist terminal operators in deciding whether or not to make the investment. Statistical and simulation methodologies are developed to better understand the availability of yard cranes versus truck turn time. The second measure is implementing a truck appointment system to regulate the number of trucks into the terminal. To this end, this research seeks to assist terminal operators in evaluating the consequences of limiting truck arrivals into the terminals. Furthermore, this research develops a methodology to assist terminal operators in implementing the truck appointment system, should they decided to have one.

Ircha, Michael C., *Characteristics of Tomorrow's Successful Port*, The AIMS Atlantica Papers #4, Atlantic Institute for Market Studies (AIMS), Halifax, Canada, January 2006.

Abstract:
There are several key attributes for a port's success in the container trade. The first is geographic location. Second, ports seeking to serve mega container ships must be accessible to them. Third, container hub ports must have and maintain a reputation for continued high productivity in terms of ship turnaround time and truck/rail car turnaround time. Fourth, container hub ports need efficient intermodal linkages (road, rail, and short sea shipping) to ensure containers are moved through the terminal quickly to reach their final inland destinations. Finally, all of these attributes must be achieved economically such that the rates and tariffs charged for container moves through the port and the terminal remain competitive. All of this is not an easy task, but it is an essential one if Canadian container ports wish to remain key players in supporting the continued development of the North American economy.

Jones, Elizabeth G., and C. Michael Walton, "Managing Containers in a Marine Terminal: Assessing Information Needs", *Transportation Research Record*, Number 1782, Paper Number 02-4058, 2002.

Abstract:
The research addresses questions about how intelligent transportation systems technologies that are being used to track and manage containers in transit can also be used to manage the stacked storage of containers in marine terminals. The research focuses on import container storage. The objective is to assess whether and how more accurate and timely information about the departure times of containers can be used to more efficiently and effectively manage import containers in stacked storage. An "informed" import storage strategy along with performance analyses of this strategy in relation to typical storage strategies used by ports is presented. The strategy for organizing import stacked storage is described. The study methodology used and subsequent analysis of these options regarding performance and economics follow. Results indicate that using a reservation system similar to the crescent system used by the port of New Orleans would significantly reduce import container–handling efforts. The system would enable a port operator to gather enough information about when import containers would leave the port to allow careful ordering of import container storage, which would result in reduced handling.

Kumar, Shashi, "User Charges for Port Cost Recovery: The US Harbour Maintenance Tax Controversy," *International Journal of Maritime Economics*, Vol. 4, 2002, p. 149-163.

Abstract:
The US incurs significant costs in order to maintain its ports and harbours. The harbour maintenance tax, introduced in 1986 under the Reagan-era overall initiative to cut back the average tax-burden, has been controversial since its inception. Its imposition on US exports was declared illegal by the Supreme Court. A proposal by the Clinton administration to introduce a harbour services user fee did not gain the support of stakeholders and thus the earlier status quo continues today with the nation's trading partners protesting vehemently. The paper analyses recent US Army Corps of Engineers data on harbour maintenance expenses in the Port of New York and New Jersey and proposes a simple yet realistic user fee model, radically different from any previous proposal, that would comply with the US Supreme Court's constitutionality test while imposing a relatively minor burden on port users. In addition, using the US as an example, the paper contributes to the general discussion on infrastructure pricing and cost recovery through user charges and in this way it addresses, albeit on the fringe, broader public policy issues such as those of mandated taxes and private versus public interest.

Langen, Peter W., *The Performance of Seaport Clusters: A Framework to Analyze Cluster Performance and an Application to the Seaport Clusters of Durban, Rotterdam and the Lower Mississippi*, PhD Dissertation, Erasmus Research Institute of Management, Erasmus University Rotterdam, 2003.

Abstract:
Surprisingly perhaps, the cluster concept has hardly been used to analyze seaports, even though port activities are geographically concentrated in a limited number of regions, mainly because geographical conditions are favorable in some regions. These regions attract substantial numbers of port related firms. Therefore, ports can be regarded as 'text-book cases' of clustering (see Fujita and Mori, 1996). Port related economic activities are of substantial importance for the regional economy in many port regions. In this dissertation the cluster concept is applied to seaports, to enhance the understanding of the performance of (seaport) clusters.

Leachman, Rob, *Port and Modal Elasticity Studies*, Leachman and Associates, Piedmont, CA for Southern California Association of Governments, Los Angeles, CA, available at: http://www.scag.ca.gov/goodsmove/pdf/FinalElasticityReport0905rev1105.pdf, last accessed: March 28, 2007, Sept 8, 2005.

Abstract:
This study determined the economic viability and impact on demand for San Pedro Bay Port services of assessing additional port user fees to fund the improvements to transportation infrastructure likely required to insure efficient and environmentally sound access to the ports. Today such user fees already exist in the form of fees for the Alameda Corridor rail line. Other major infrastructure improvements may be required to accommodate further traffic growth, and user fees are one possibility for funding such improvements. The Port and Modal Elasticity Study analyses the long-run elasticity of port demands as a function of access fees, determining what levels of fees would induce traffic diversion to other ports or induce shifts in modal shares (truck vs. rail) at the San Pedro Bay (SPB) Ports. These shifts also may depend upon the point in the overall logistics supply chain at which user fees are assessed.

Luo, Meifeng and Thomas A. Grigalunas, "A Spatial-Economic Multimodal Transportation Simulation Model for US Coastal Container Ports," manuscript, July 18, 2002.

Abstract:
This paper develops and applies a spatial-economic, multi-modal container transportation simulation model for US coastal container ports. The model is validated and then used to evaluate the impact on port demand from varying port use fees, i.e., to evaluate the responsiveness (price elasticity) of demand to varying port use fees. The paper draws upon results from the Ph.D. dissertation of Luo (2002), which is part of a multi-year study by the authors and their colleagues at the University of Rhode Island and the Korea Maritime Institute from 1999 to now (Grigalunas et al, 2001). The underlying theoretical framework is based on fundamental microeconomic theory and assumes shippers minimize the total general cost of moving containers from sources to markets. We apply the model to estimate annual container transportation service demand for major container ports in the United States (US). First, we outline the model formulation, focusing on the model and the underlying economic reasoning. We also provide a very brief introduction to the assumptions, computational algorithm, and the software architecture. Then, we explain the data used in applying the model, including trade data, transportation networks, and economic variables. After that, we use the estimated container transportation flow origin-destination (OD) matrix to illustrate the model simulation results. All models, including the one presented here, are simplifications, and we stress that the model remains a work in progress. Limitations in the modelling approach, needed refinements, ongoing work, and future directions are briefly described in the final section.

Makkar, Jagmeet, "Commercial Aspects of Shipping: Market Dynamics (Part 3)", *Sailor Today,* November 2005, p. 60-64.

Abstract:
In the October issue, we looked at demand and supply models and their short run interaction to arrive at freight rates. This month, we will review the effect of port congestion, scrapping and increased supply on the demand and supply model after a quick revision of the equilibrium freight rate.

Malchow, Matthew B., *An Analysis of Port Selection*, Ph.D. Dissertation, University of California, Berkeley, Department of Engineering, available at: http://repositories.cdlib.org/its/ds/UCB-ITS-DS-2001-3, Last Accessed: Feb 16, 2007, Spring 2001.

Abstract:
The objective of this research is to study the competition among ports. In particular we study the relation between port characteristics and port market share of maritime traffic. Maritime carriers make two primary decisions that affect ports. In the long-term, they assign vessels to routes. In the short-term, they assign each shipment to a vessel and, with that vessel, a port. In this research, we assume that vessel schedules are fixed and model the assignment of shipments as a function of the attributes that describe each port. For a carrier, some assignments are simpler than other assignments. Each assignment should, however, take into account the same criteria. We begin by examining the scheduling of vessels for its effect on the assignment of shipments. We measure the impact of being a vessel's first or last port of call on a port's market share, and we discuss factors that might influence these schedules. We then examine the assignment to ports for exports of various commodity types as a function of geographic location (oceanic and inland distances), port characteristics (vessel capacity and port charges), and characteristics of vessel schedules (frequency and the order of visits). We use a multinomial choice model to analyze port choice. We find that the most significant factors are the geographic factors, which are beyond port control. The factors that ports can influence directly appear to be of far less significance. We also find that the choice processes vary with commodity type as well as carrier. The decisions are also found to differ between local and discretionary cargo. Our findings could affect decisions made by port managers as well as carriers or shippers. With the recognition of geographic advantages, port managers could focus marketing more effectively. Recognizing the impact of each carrier's schedules, they could suggest changes to carriers presently visiting the port or recruit new carriers to use present facilities more efficiently. Port managers could also evaluate more effectively investments designed to increase market share. Facilities or technologies could be incremented with a more accurate vision of future traffic levels at individual ports.

Martonosi, Susan E., David S. Ortiz, and Henry H. Willis, "Evaluating the Viability of 100 per cent Container Inspection at America's Ports," *The Economic Impacts of Terrorist Attacks*, Edward Elgar Publishing, February 2006.

Abstract:
In this chapter, we perform a cost-benefit analysis of implementing a policy of scanning 100 per cent of incoming containers at US ports, exploring issues of technological cost and performance, and we examine the minimum threat necessary to justify the costs of particular inspection proposals.

Meersman, E., E. Van de Voorde and T. Vanelslander, *Port Pricing: Considerations on Economic Principles and Marginal Costs*, European Journal of Transport and Infrastructure Research, Vol. 3:4, January 2004, p. 371-386.

Abstract:
Pricing by ports and operators within ports is considered quite a complex and untransparant matter, and as such it is sometimes perceived as archaic. This often results in debates about subsidies, captive markets and the dredging and deepening of maritime access routes, raising questions concerning potential distortion of competition and/or abuse of monopolistic power. This paper starts from the most important scientific literature on port pricing (and port competition), and adds new empirical results while calculating the marginal cost of a port call. A distinction is made between four elements of marginal costs in port operations, being costs for provision of infrastructure, costs associated with the use of the transport mode, costs for supplying port services, and external costs. This material may constitute the basis for a meaningful debate on the implementation of a pricing approach that is grounded on the marginal cost principle.

Meersman, E. E. Van de Voorde and T. Vanelslander, "Port Pricing Issues: Considerations on Economic Principles, Competition and Wishful Thinking," IMPRINT-Europe Thematic Network Conference, *Implementing Reform on Transport Pricing: Identifying Mode-Specific Issues"*, Brussels, available at: http://www.imprint-eu.org/public/Themaccess.htm, last accessed: Marcy 28, 2007, May 14-15, 2002.

Abstract:
Pricing by ports and operators within ports is historically determined. It is often quite a complex and untransparent matter, and as such is sometimes perceived as archaic. Debates on overt or covert subsidies, captive markets and the need to constantly dredge and deepen maritime access routes undoubtedly raise questions in the minds of those who are wary of potential distortion of competition and/or abuse of monopolistic power but, at the same time, have little or no insight into the operating of ports. This paper deals with the issue of pricing for port calls and port services. We shall deal consecutively with the questions of what a port is exactly and how port services and transshipment should be defined. After a brief survey of the most important scientific literature on port pricing, we shall dwell upon some empirical aspects. We shall consider prevailing pricing practice in various ports, econometric estimations of price elasticity, and the calculation/simulation of marginal port call costs and transshipment costs. In this manner, we intend to achieve the objectives of IMPRINT-EUROPE, i.e. to "develop recommendations for how to implement transport pricing reform based on the principles of marginal cost pricing."

Monaco, Kristen and Jeffrey Cohen, *Ports and Highways Infrastructure Investment and Inter-state Spatial Spillovers*, METRANS, Project 05-04, available at: http://www.metrans.org/research/, last accessed: March 28, 2007, March 2006.

Abstract:
U.S. ports serve a vital role in the nations' supply chain and international trade. While the areas surrounding these ports bear the external costs of port expansion (congestion, air pollution, noise pollution) the benefits from port activity are felt by other regions that do not bear these costs. The purpose of this study is to assess the role that transportation infrastructure plays in production and employment in the manufacturing industry. Using state-level data from the 48 contiguous states, we model manufacturing production and cost, incorporating state and local investment in port and highway infrastructure as variables in the model. We find that states benefit from increasing their own ports infrastructure, but do not benefit from increased infrastructure in neighboring states. We also find that highways and ports infrastructure are neither complements nor substitutes.

Mongelluzzo, Bill, "Nuclear attack on LA-LB would cause $1 trillion economic impact: Rand", *Journal of Commerce,* August 16, 2006.

Abstract:
A nuclear bomb detonated in a container at the Port of Long Beach would immediately kill 60,000 persons and cause an estimated $1 trillion in economic damage, according to a Rand Corp. study.

Mongelluzzo, Bill, "Pressed for Time," *Journal of Commerce,* September 11, 2006.

Abstract:

Few things cause more heartburn for ocean carriers than missing a Panama Canal transit appointment. And that goes for shippers, too. The path between the Atlantic and Pacific is a key part of carrier schedules and shipper supply chains, and this year has been a rough one for providers and users of all-water services that rely on the canal.

Mongelluzzo, Bill, "Red Alert: As Government Listens, Port Interests Warm of Chaos under TWIC," *Journal of Commerce*, June 26, 2006.

Abstract:

Marine terminal operators, harbor trucking companies and labor unions are preparing for the launch of the Transportation Worker Identification Credential program with a doomsday vision. They foresee lengthy delays at terminal gates and an exodus of workers who can't qualify for TWIC cards because of immigration status or criminal records.

Mongelluzzo, Bill, "TGIF? Not in Southern California," *Journal of Commerce*, February 20, 2006.

Abstract:

Friday afternoon traffic jams in Southern California are legendary, but congestion on the freeways can't compare to the vessel traffic that pours into the ports of Los Angeles and Long Beach each weekend. "Friday and Saturday is crunch time," says Doug Tilden, chief executive of Marine Terminals Corp. Trans-Pacific carriers build their schedules to fit restrictions such as factory cutoff times in Asia and no-work practices on Sundays in Japanese ports. As a result, virtually all ships seem to be on the same schedule, which has them arriving at the port of Los Angeles-Long Beach in a narrow 48-hour window.

Sjostrom, William, "Ocean Shipping Cartels: A Survey," *Review of Network Economics*, Vol. 3:2, June 2004.

Abstract:

Liner shipping has been characterized by collusive agreements, called shipping conferences, since its founding in the mid-nineteenth century. This article surveys the competing models of shipping conferences, including monopolizing cartels and destructive competition models, and reviews a variety of their practices to see how much light they can shed on the profitability and efficiency of conferences.

Talley, Wayne K., An Economic Theory of the Port, Maritime Institute, Department of Economics, Old Dominion University, available at: http://bpa.odu.edu/port/research/porttheoryA.doc, last accessed: March 28, 2007.

Abstract:
This chapter presents an economic theory of the cargo port. It is assumed that the port handles two types of cargo, bulk and container, and has the economic objective of maximizing annual throughput (of bulk and container cargoes) subject to a minimum profit constraint. If the port is owned by government, this profit constraint may be zero (where port revenue equals cost) or a maximum deficit (where port revenue is less than cost) that is to be subsidized by government. In the following section, the basic economic model of the port is presented, followed by a discussion of port operating options. Then, a discussion of extending the model to incorporate port ship and vehicle congestion is presented, followed by a discussion of port cost efficiency. Then, the applicability of the theory to port performance evaluation and empirical research is discussed. Finally, a summary is presented.

Tiwari, Piyush, Hidekazu Itoh, and Masayuki Doi, "Containerized Cargo Shipper's Behavior in China: A Discrete Choice Analysis," *Journal of Transportation and Statistics*, Vol. 6:1, November 2003.

Abstract:
Shippers choose ports for export or import of goods based on a number of variables, including location, preferences for particular shipping line services, and facilities offered. A huge port infrastructure investment is necessary to attract shippers, and ports compete with each other for business. This paper models the port and shipping line choice behavior of shippers in China, using a shipper-level database obtained from a 1998 survey of containerized cargo shippers. We used a discrete choice model where each shipper chooses among 10 shipping line and port combinations and makes decisions based on various shipper and port characteristics. This paper incorporates the shipping line choice behavior through model specification by nesting the choices in a hierarchical fashion where shippers choose from Chinese and non-Chinese shipping lines and then from ports or vice versa. The results indicate that the distance of the shipper from the port, the number of ship calls at the port, the efficiency of the port infrastructure, and the number of routes offered at the port strongly influence decisions to use a port.

Tovar, Beatriz, Sergio Jara-Díaz, and Lourdes Trujillo, "Production and Cost Functions and Their Application to the Port Sector: A Literature Survey," *World Bank Policy Research Working Paper*, Number 3123, available at: http://econ.worldbank.org, August, 2003.

Abstract:
Seaports provide multiple services to ships, cargo, and passengers. These services can be performed by a combination of public and private initiatives. Usually, the role of public sector institutions is to regulate and supervise private firms. In performing that task public sector institutions need to know firms' cost structure deeply. This paper offers a review of the literature about ports' cost structure and of its implications for regulation. The paper argues that the operation of port terminals should be analysed by means of multiproduct theory. This approach allows the calculation of several cost indicators (economies of scale, scope, and so forth) which are key tools to help regulators.

Traffic World, Record Containers Flowing Smoothly, *Traffic World,* October 9, 2006.

Abstract:
A key shipper group says freight is moving smoothly without delays through key United States ports even as imports reach new records this peak season.

United Nations, *Comparative Analysis of Port Tariffs in The ESCAP Region*, Document Number ST/ESCAP/2190, 2002.

Abstract:
Ports of the ESCAP region have long-established tariff structures. These are contained in published schedules, which vary in length from a few pages to more than one hundred. Some tariffs are extremely complex while others are relatively simple. There is, however, an increasing desire on the part of port users for greater transparency in the billing of port services. This highlights the need for more easily understandable and comparable tariff structures. In order to address these issues, the ESCAP secretariat undertook a comparative study of port tariffs across a significant number of ports in the region. The study was carried out as a joint project under the Memorandum of Understanding, which was signed in 1998, between ESCAP and the Korea Maritime Institute.

U.S. Department of Homeland Security, Transportation Security Administration, *Transportation Worker Identification Credential: Overview*, TWIC Overview Brief 2.0, available at: http://www.maritimedelriv.com/Port_Security/TSA/TSA_Port_Security.htm, last accessed: March 28, 2007, May 2006.

Abstract:
Vision: Improve the security of identity management by establishing a national system wide common credential, universally acceptable across all transportation modes, for all personnel whose duties require unescorted physical and/or logical access to secure areas of the transportation system. Goals: -Improve security -Enhance commerce -Protect personal privacy

U.S. Department of Transportation, Maritime Administration, *Report to Congress on the Performance of Ports and the Intermodal System*, available at: http://www.marad.dot.gov/publications/ports.htm, last accessed: March 28, 2007, June, 2005.

Abstract:
In this report, MARAD provides an assessment of the conditions at commercial ports, and the movement of military cargo through the intermodal system during the Operation Iraqi Freedom (OIF) buildup. MARAD's assessment includes the performance of the major components of the intermodal system: waterside, port/terminal intermodal interface, and landside movements. Particular emphasis is given to the ability of the nation's commercial freight transportation infrastructure to handle an unexpected surge in cargo during a military deployment, such as OIF.

Ward, Andrew, "Congested ports warning for US importers," *Financial Times,* March 2, 2005.

Abstract:
US importers can expect another year of supply bottlenecks and rising supply-chain costs because of congestion in west coast ports, transport industry executives and analysts have warned.

Waterfront Coalition, *National Marine Container Transportation System: A Call To Action,* Available at: www.portmod.org, last accessed: March 28, 2007, May 2005.

World Bank, *Port Reform Toolkit*, Available at: http://www.ppiaf.org/Port/toolkit.html, Last Accessed: March 28, 2007.

Abstract:
The port sector has radically changed over the past two centuries. During the 19th century and first half of the 20th century ports tended to be instruments of state or colonial powers and port access and egress was regarded as a means to control markets. Competition between ports was minimal and port-related costs were relatively insignificant in comparison to the high cost of ocean transport and inland transport. As a result, there was little incentive to improve port efficiency. How times have changed! Most ports today are competing with one another on a global scale and, with the tremendous gains in productivity in ocean transport achieved over the past several decades, ports are now perceived to be the remaining controllable component in improving the efficiency of ocean transport logistics. This has generated the drive today to improve port efficiency, lower cargo handling costs and integrate port services with other components of the global distribution network. Because of the capital intensity of such efficiency improvements, these have also generated the drive to unbind ports from bureaucratic control of public entities and encourage private sector operation of a wide range of port related activities.

APPENDIX B: U.S. CODE OF FEDERAL REGULATIONS PERTAINING TO PORT OPERATIONS AND U.S. COAST GUARD JURISDICTION

This section examines the intersection between the regulatory authority granted the Coast Guard in the Code of Federal Regulations (CFR) and the particular impacts that its authority may have on port operations. In general, Coast Guard regulations do not directly affect port operations. The principal exception relates to maritime security regulations, which were expanded by the Maritime Transportation Security Act (MTSA) of 2002.

Coast Guard regulatory authority is found in CFR Titles 33 and 46, which were examined for this report. Generally, Title 33 addresses security, environmental protection, and some aspects of vessel operations, while Title 46 addresses marine safety on the whole. Many regulations are aimed at specific vessel types, particularly in Title 46. None specifically address container ships, and those that are vessel-specific do not apply to container ships. The Coast Guard does not regulate the construction or maintenance of the shipping containers, themselves. Many regulations apply to all ship types, addressing navigation and safety. New or enhanced provisions in these areas would not seem to directly affect port operations, as their impact ends both physically and operationally at the edge of the water. Examples include:

- Ship's fire safety regulations prescribe structural fire protection, fire detection, and fire suppression systems onboard, but do not address shoreside (port) firefighting capabilities in any way.
- Piping for oil transfer, whether ship's fuel or oil cargoes, is regulated by the Coast Guard up to the "flange," that is, the meeting point of ship and port piping. There are physical and operational standards that enhance safety (for instance, the proper method for grounding transfer pipes to prevent electrostatic discharge) but Coast Guard regulation have no direct effect on the port.
- Stability regulations ensure that the crew will keep the ship within accepted minimum safe margins, including during loading and unloading of cargo. Compliance with this most basic safety regulation has no effect on the port, unless, of course, the crew fails and the ship heels violently or capsizes.

Environmental protection regulations address shipboard equipment and operations. There are also several emergency planning and response regulations (for example, for oil or hazardous substance spills on the water) for both vessels and facilities. The latter, of course, affect container ports, but only for spills on the water. Emergency planning is not likely to effect port operations or costs, and the Coast Guard authority as On Scene Coordinator (OSC) during a pollution event is rare and, when exercised, episodic, rather than routine. Otherwise, Federal (through the Environmental Protection Agency), state, and local regulations address the port landside environmental compliance issues.

Port and vessel security regulations are described in 33 CFR Part 6, with authority vested in Sector Commanders, with the power to ensure security in extreme situations. The 33 CFR Parts 101-105, regulations arising from MTSA, are more specific than those in 33 CFR Part 6, but are more suggestive than prescriptive. A detailed list of the parts in 33 CFR and their applicability to port operations can be found in Table 9.

The inputs required to determine the effects of new or modified regulations are likely to require case-by-case analysis in order to properly assess the effect of a particular rulemaking. That is, the provisions of, say, a new security regulation would have to be analyzed for their particular effects in terms of time and cost. As described elsewhere in this report, a range of methods of primary and secondary data analysis, including operations assessment through site visits and literature reviews, and input from experts, will be used to characterize the changes to port attributes caused by proposed regulations.

Table 9: U.S. Code of Federal Regulations Pertaining to the U.S. Coast Guard

Part	Descriptor	Affect container port operations	Comments
Subchapter A – General			
1	General provisions	N	
2	Jurisdiction	N	
3	Coast Guard areas, districts, marine inspection zones, and captain of the port zones	N	
4	OMB control numbers assigned pursuant to the Paperwork Reduction Act	N	
5	Coast Guard Auxiliary	N	
6	Protection and security of vessels, harbors, and waterfront facilities	Y	General authority for port security; personnel, HAZMAT, security zones
8	United States Coast Guard Reserve	N	
13	Decorations, medals, ribbons and similar devices	N	
17	United States Coast Guard general gift fund	N	
19	Waivers of navigation and vessel inspection laws and regulations	N	
20	Rules of practice, procedure, and evidence for formal administrative proceedings of the Coast Guard	N	
23	Distinctive markings for Coast Guard vessels and aircraft	N	
25	Claims	N	
26	Vessel bridge-to-bridge radiotelephone regulations	N	
27	Adjustment of civil monetary penalties for inflation	N	
Subchapter B – Military Personnel			
40	Cadets of the Coast Guard	N	
45	Enlistment of personnel	N	
49	Payment of amounts due mentally incompetent Coast Guard personnel	N	
50	Coast Guard Retiring Review Board	N	
51	Coast Guard Discharge Review Board	N	
52	Board for Correction of Military Records of the Coast Guard	N	
53	Coast Guard whistleblower protection	N	
54	Allotments from active duty pay for certain support obligations	N	
55	Child Development Services	N	
60	[Reserved]	N	
Subchapter C -- Aids to Navigation			

Part	Descriptor	Affect container port operations	Comments
62	United States aids to navigation system	N	
64	Marking of structures, sunken vessels and other obstructions	N	
66	Private aids to navigation	N	
67	Aids to navigation on artificial islands and fixed structures	N	
70	Interference with or damage to aids to navigation	N	
72	Marine information	N	
74	Charges for Coast Guard aids to navigation work	N	
76	Sale and transfer of aids to navigation equipment	N	
Subchapter D -- International Navigation Rules			
	Note: Application of the 72 COLREGS to territories and possessions	N	
80	COLREGS demarcation lines	N	
81	72 COLREGS: Implementing Rules	N	
82	72 COLREGS: Interpretative Rules	N	
84	Annex I: Positioning and technical details of lights and shapes	N	
85	Annex II: Additional signals for fishing vessels fishing in close proximity	N	
86	Annex III: Technical details of sound signal appliances	N	
87	Annex IV: Distress signals	N	
88	Annex V: Pilot rules	N	
Subchapter E -- Inland Navigation Rules			
89	Inland navigation rules: implementing rules	N	
90	Inland rules: Interpretative rules	N	
Subchapter F -- Vessel Operating Regulations			
95	Operating a vessel while under the influence of alcohol or a dangerous drug	N	
96	Rules for the safe operation of vessels and safety management systems	Y	National and international certification for the company's and vessel's safety management system
Subchapter G -- Regattas and Marine Parades			
100	Safety of life on navigable waters	N	
Subchapter H -- General Maritime Security			
101	Maritime Security: General	Y	
102	Maritime Security: National maritime transportation security [Reserved]	Y	
103	Maritime security: Area maritime security	Y	
104	Maritime security: Vessels	Y	
105	Maritime security: Facilities	Y	
106	Marine Security: Outer Continental Shelf (OCS) facilities	N	
107	National Vessel and Facility Control Measures and Limited Access Areas	Y	
Subchapter I — Anchorages			
109	General	N	
110	Anchorage regulations	N	
Subchapter J — Bridges			
114	General	N	
115	Bridge locations and clearances; administrative procedures	N	
116	Alteration of unreasonably obstructive bridges	N	
117	Drawbridge operation regulations	N	
118	Bridge lighting and other signals	N	
Subchapter K -- Security of Vessels			
120	Security of passenger vessels	N	
125	Identification credentials for persons requiring access to waterfront facilities or vessels	Y	
126	Handling of dangerous cargo at waterfront facilities	Y	
127	Waterfront facilities handling liquefied natural gas and liquefied hazardous gas	N	
Subchapter L -- Security of passenger terminals			
128	Security of passenger terminals	N	

Part	Descriptor	Affect container port operations	Comments
Subchapter M -- Oil spill liability trust fund			
133	Oil spill liability trust fund; State access	N	
135	Offshore oil pollution compensation fund	N	
136	Oil spill liability trust fund; claims procedures; designation of source; and advertisement	N	
138	Financial responsibility for water pollution (vessels)	N	
Subchapter N – Outer Continental Shelf Facilities			
140	General	N	
141	Personnel	N	
142	Workplace safety and health	N	
143	Design and equipment	N	
144	Lifesaving appliances	N	
145	Fire-fighting equipment	N	
146	Operations	N	
147	Safety zones	N	
Subchapter NN – Deepwater Ports			
148	Deepwater ports: General	N	
149	Deepwater ports: Design, construction, and equipment	N	
150	Deepwater ports: Operations	N	
Subchapter O -- Vessels carrying oil, noxious liquid substances, garbage, municipal or commercial waste, and ballast water			
151	Vessels carrying oil, noxious liquid substances, garbage, municipal or commercial waste, and ballast water	Y	
153	Control of pollution by oil and hazardous substances, discharge removal	N	
154	Facilities transferring oil or hazardous material in bulk	N	
155	Oil or hazardous material pollution prevention regulations for vessels	N	
156	Oil and hazardous material transfer operations	N	
157	Rules for the protection of the marine environment relating to tank vessels carrying oil in bulk	N	
158	Reception facilities for oil, noxious liquid substances, and garbage	N	
159	Marine sanitation devices	N	
Subchapter P –Ports and Waterways Safety			
160	Ports and waterways safety--general	N	Assume compliance of shipping companies with these basic navigational safety regulations.
161	Vessel traffic management	N	
162	Inland waterways navigation regulations	N	
163	Towing of barges	N	
164	Navigation safety regulations	N	
165	Regulated navigation areas and limited access areas	N	
166	Shipping safety fairways	N	
167	Offshore traffic separation schemes	N	
168	Escort requirements for certain tankers	N	
169	Ship reporting systems	N	
	Index to Subchapter P		
173	Vessel numbering and casualty and accident reporting	N	
174	State numbering and casualty reporting systems	N	
175	Equipment requirements	N	
177	Correction of especially hazardous conditions	N	
179	Defect notification	N	
181	Manufacturer requirements	N	
183	Boats and associated equipment	N	
184-186	[Reserved]	NA	
187	Vessel identification system	N	

APPENDIX C: THE DELPHI TECHNIQUE

A natural approach to use to build estimates when there is a knowledgeable group available is the Delphi technique. The Delphi technique is a process used to elicit information or judgments from participants through an iterative information exchange process. The participants in the Delphi process can be experts or stakeholders with a knowledge of or interest in the information being gathered.

Operationally, the Delphi technique does not require that the participants be co-located. The iterative information exchange process that is at the heart of the Delphi technique can be accomplished in person, through virtual meetings, or in written form.

A team or individual functioning as a coordinator manages the Delphi process. The coordinator creates an initial questionnaire, which is then sent to all participants. The responses are collected and reviewed by the coordinator. Based on those responses, a new questionnaire is developed and sent to all of the participants. The process continues with additional questionnaires that are always based on the results of the previous questionnaire until consensus is achieved. If consensus cannot be achieved (or if consensus is not the goal) the coordinator can achieve resolution in a variety of ways, including voting. To help ensure the true opinions of all participants are obtained, all responses are confidential.

The general theme of the questions remains the same in each subsequent questionnaire. For instance, an initial questionnaire might be sent to port security officers asking the general question "What changes might one see at a container port after regulating container stack height?" The first questionnaire would be open ended and participants would be expected to list the methods that they consider effective. The second questionnaire might list the methods submitted and ask for comments concerning the strengths and weaknesses of each, while still encouraging additional methods to be submitted. A third questionnaire might include summarized responses from the second. After the third, the coordinator might send out a request to rank the methods according to their relative effectiveness. The coordinator would then send out a summary of the "vote," allowing participants to benefit from shared knowledge among colleagues about port impacts while the coordinator obtains data for further analysis or modeling.

While the Delphi technique can be very effective, it can also fail for a number of reasons. Those include:

- Imposing the coordinator's opinions or preconceptions on the process
- Ignoring and not exploring disagreements that arise in the responses
- Failing to properly summarize and present the responses
- Failing to choose a proper group for exploring the question of interest

The last problem can arise in any situation, of course, and is not limited necessarily to the Delphi technique.

APPENDIX D: ANALYTICAL HIERARCHY PROCESS

Decision-making often includes the weighing of multiple criteria, evaluation of trade-offs and coming to consensus as a group. The application of consistent scoring mechanisms can introduce subtle errors into analysis. The need to use both quantitative and qualitative information often characterizes real-world cases and distinguishes them from the simpler examples in textbooks. These features often lead to the implementation of some form of the Analytic Hierarchy Process (AHP). The fact that it succeeds in performing relative rankings and other complex tasks in a straightforward manner may explain why DM suggests that such methods be used in decision-making.

AHP can be characterized as a multi-criteria decision technique in which qualitative factors are of prime of importance. A model of the problem is developed using a hierarchical representation, that is, various sub-goals are generally specified that contribute to the top goal. At the top of the hierarchy is the overall goal or prime objective one is seeking to fulfill. The succeeding lower levels then represent the progressive decomposition of the problem. The knowledgeable parties (e.g., individual team members) complete a pair-wise comparison of all entries in each level relative to each of the entries in the next higher level of the hierarchy. The composition of these judgments fixes the relative priority of the entities at the lowest level (e.g. individual team members) relative to achieving the top-most objective.

This approach has been used in aviation safety applications, hazmat shipping evaluations,[11] and other transportation and non-transportation related fields.

Software for AHP implementations includes commercial packages such as Expert Choice 11 and CRIT 2001.[13] It is also straightforward to implement the software as a database application such as Access, or in a spreadsheet. The basic calculation process is well documented in many volumes, especially those by Saaty, who originated the approach.[14]

---

[11] Assessing the Impacts from the Introduction of Advanced Transport Telematics Technologies in Hazardous Materials Fleet Management, by G.G. Dografos and G. Androutsopoulos, Athens University of Economics and Business, Department of Management Science and Marketing, undated.
[13] See, http://www.expertchoice.com/software, and http://www.arlingsoft.com, respectively.
[14] See, for example, Thomas Saaty, Decision Making for Leaders, 19??, RWS Publications, Pittsburgh.